TALES OF LORD SHIVA

Neither am I mind, nor intelligence,
Nor ego, nor thought,
Nor am I ears or the tongue or the nose or the eyes,
Nor am I earth or sky or air or the light,
But I am Shiva the eternal Bliss.

- Nirvana Shatakam, Adi Shankaracharya

Quantic books

English
TALES OF LORD SHIVA
Retold by Yadu Vijayakrishnan

Published by
Quantic Creatives Private Limited.
Corporate Office: Quantic Nexus
TC 22/2459, SRL-A 68, Sankar Road, Sasthamangalam,
Thiruvananthapuram, Kerala 695010
Tel: 8289816366 | 8590011447
www.quanticcreatives.in

First published in 2025

Cover Design by Yadu Vijayakrishnan

Layout: Qlife Infotech

ISBN: 978-81-981675-6-9

Price: ₹ 350.00

TALES OF
LORD SHIVA

Yadu Vijayakrishnan

Quantic books

PREFACE

Hinduism is the oldest living religion in the world. In contrast, the ancient religions of Egypt, Greece, and Persia have long vanished, their extinction occurring before the medieval age. Despite being rich in mythology and ritual, these faiths could not withstand the test of time. However, it would be incorrect to claim that they were simply destroyed by the rise of Abrahamic religions. If that were true, how did Hinduism endure repeated invasions from the West since the 8th century CE? Furthermore, Hinduism has outlasted and surpassed offshoots like Buddhism and Jainism.

This resilience of Hinduism can be attributed to its rich scriptures and strong oral traditions. If it had only been a religion of polytheistic rituals, it likely would have disappeared ages ago. Hinduism is not just a faith but a broad cultural and philosophical tradition, encompassing numerous schools of thought, arts, and sciences. In fact, the term "Hinduism" itself was coined by outsiders, referring to the people of India who followed a unique way of life. If you could travel back in time and ask the people of ancient India what religion they followed, they might look confused, as the concept of "religion" as we understand it did not exist. Their practices were grounded in science and philosophy rather than a simple belief in many gods.

Like other ancient faiths, Hinduism has multiple deities, each representing various aspects of power. However, it sets itself apart through its moral teachings and profound philosophical systems. In contrast, the polytheistic religions of ancient Europe and Africa, though rich in mythology, often lacked the structured principles found in Hindu texts. While these myths may have been fascinating stories, they seldom offered deeper philosophical insights or moral frameworks.

Hinduism's distinctiveness lies in the lessons and values woven into its stories. The same text can inspire countless commentaries, revealing layers of meaning. For example, the Ramayana exists in over 120 Sanskrit versions alone. While the Ramayana and Mahabharata are often regarded as historical epics, the Puranas offer a different kind of narrative.

Among the many Puranas, eighteen are considered Maha Puranas or "Great Puranas." These include the Vishnu Purana, Bhagavata Purana, Shiva Purana, and many others, categorized into three types: Sattva (truth and purity), Rajas (passion), and Tamas (ignorance and darkness). The Shiva Purana and Linga Purana fall under the Tamas category, but this does not imply negativity. Instead, these texts are meant to uplift those in a state of ignorance and guide them toward enlightenment, much like a potent medicine for the soul.

You may wonder how mere stories can lead to spiritual liberation. Think of it like a lesson from your early school days. Imagine your teacher trying to explain that 1 + 1 = 2. To help you understand, they might say, "You have one apple, and your father gives you another—now you have two apples." The Puranas function similarly, using stories to illustrate deeper truths. In one version of a story, one character performs an action, while in another version, a different character does the same. But the core moral remains unchanged, just as the equation 1 + 1 = 2.

These stories were passed down through oral tradition, with elders narrating them to younger generations. Even though that practice has become rare, modern printing and media have kept these stories alive, ensuring that they remain relevant. The role of the Puranas in preserving Hinduism and the Sanatana way of life cannot be overstated.

The Tales of Lord Shiva is a collection of stories from the Shiva

Purana, Linga Purana, Brahma Purana and Aithihyamala. These stories are presented in chronological order, from the creation of the universe to events in the 18th and 19th centuries. The book also explores the twelve Jyotirlinga temples and includes rare stories about Lord Shiva not found online. I hope you find these tales engaging and enlightening. A version with commentaries and illustrations is also in progress.

CONTENTS

1.	Origins	9
2.	Shiva's Attire	13
3.	Samudra Manthan	16
4.	Shiva and Sati	21
5.	The Daksha Yaga	26
6.	The Birth of Mars	38
7.	Rise of Tarakasura	41
8.	Shiva and Parvati	46
9.	Kartikeya	52
10.	Ganesh	55
11.	Andhaka	60
12.	Ashokasundari	66
13.	Shastha	69
14.	Jalandhara	74
15.	Raktaja	79
16.	Gangadhara	83
17.	Kali and Raktabija	87
18.	The Fall of Tripura	95
19.	Agni	104
20.	Hanuman	108
21.	Pandava's Past Lives	112
22.	Kirata Avatar	116
23.	Outset of Shivalayottam	123
24.	Somnath	126
25.	Mahakaleshwar	130
26.	Kedarnath	133
27.	Bhimashankar	135
28.	Vishveshwara	139
29.	Triambakeshwara	142

30.	Vaidyanath	147
31.	Nageshwar	151
32.	Rameshwar	155
33.	Ghushmeshwar	158
34.	Mallikarjuna	162
35.	Omkareshwar	165
36.	Vishnu worships Shiva	167
37.	Guruguha the Hunter	170
38.	Krishna worships Shiva	176
39.	Time Flies	179
40.	True Devotion	182
41.	Markandeya	185
42.	The King's Wish	189
43.	Murthi's Revolution	192
44.	Adi Shankara's Encounter	196
45.	The Uninvited Guests	199
46.	Spider's Venom	202
47.	Cure of a Shaiva	205
48.	Elixir for Insanity	210
49.	Change of Fate	213
50.	Life Span of Shiva	216
	GLOSSARY	219

1

ORIGINS

In the beginning, there was only darkness. It was all-encompassing, a void without shape or form. The universe had yet to be born. There were no stars, no sun, no moon, not a single spark of light, no wind or water. There was nothing, only emptiness. Yet within this nothingness, *Sat* existed. *Sat*, the eternal truth, had no form or color, no boundaries or characteristics. It was beyond description. It was neither large nor small. It simply was. This *Sat* was the embodiment of pure consciousness, a union of knowledge, bliss, and the essence of all emotions.

This formless entity is also known as *Brahman*, or *Brahma*. From its infinite potential, the *Nirakara* (formless) *Brahman* willed itself into existence. It transformed into a radiant *Jyotirlingam* - a pillar of light, a symbol of the universe itself, the *Brahmandam*. But the formless Brahman desired more. It wished for creation, for the multiplication of its essence into countless forms. And so, it decided to manifest itself in a divine form, filled with limitless wisdom, greatness, and splendour. This form was *Sada Shiva*, the eternal, the supreme embodiment of divine consciousness.

Sada Shiva, in his infinite wisdom, contemplated the creation of the cosmos. To bring forth life, he established the eternal cycle of *Srishti*, *Stiti*, and *Samhara* - Creation, Preservation, and Destruction. From the divine essence of his left side, smeared with the nectar of immortality, a being emerged. Radiant and powerful, with eyes like the blazing sun, this being stood before Sada Shiva, bowing in reverence.

The being asked, "O Lord, what name will you bestow upon me? What is my purpose? What is the task I must fulfill?"

Sada Shiva, filled with contentment, replied, "You shall be known as *Vishnu*, for your presence will be felt everywhere. You will bear many names, for you will bring prosperity to your devotees. But to discover your purpose, you must undergo deep meditation."

Vishnu, obedient to the divine will, began his penance. Ages passed, and his meditation grew more intense. So deep was his focus that his body began to sweat and his sweat filled the void, forming a vast ocean. Exhausted, Vishnu lay down upon the waters to rest. As he floated in the cosmic sea, he became known as *Narayana* - the one who rests upon the waters.

In this primordial expanse, there was no life yet, save for Narayana himself. As he slept, a magnificent lotus bloomed from his navel. Its petals shimmered like the sun, radiating beauty beyond description. From the left side of Sada Shiva's body, through the illusion of *Maya*, *BrahmaDev* was born and placed upon this divine lotus. Yet BrahmaDev, enveloped in ignorance, did not know who created him, nor his purpose.

"If I descend the stem of this lotus, perhaps I can find my creator," BrahmaDev thought, and so he began his journey. But no matter how far he traveled, the stem seemed endless. Defeated, BrahmaDev paused, and in the stillness, he heard a voice: "Meditate!"

For twelve long years, BrahmaDev meditated, seeking his creator. At the end of his penance, Vishnu appeared before him, glowing with divine light. BrahmaDev opened his eyes and the two began a conversation. However, their discussion soon evolved into an argument, and they forgot their quest for truth.

Suddenly, a towering pillar of fire erupted before them, stretching infinitely in both directions, its beginning and end unseen. Overwhelmed, they asked, "What is this? Where does it come from? Where does it end?"

United in curiosity, they set aside their quarrel and began their quest to find the limits of the fiery column. Vishnu travelled downward, BrahmaDev upward, but neither could find its source. Realizing the futility of their search, they understood that this endless pillar of light was none other than the *Jyotirlinga*, the embodiment of the supreme divine. Humbled, they prayed, "O Lord, reveal yourself to us. Let us behold your true form."

For a hundred years, they meditated, their egos dissolving into the pure desire to see the origin of the Jyotirlinga. And then, the universe resonated with the sacred sound of *Aum*, and a radiant figure emerged. *Parameswara*, the Lord of All, Lord Shiva himself.

"My dear gods," Shiva spoke, "I am pleased with your devotion. You must worship me as you first saw me, in the form of the Jyotirlinga. By doing so, you will gain unparalleled power. You were both born from my essence, and you shall be revered by all. BrahmaDev, I grant you the divine responsibility of creation. You will populate the universe with beings of all forms and intellects. Vishnu, you shall preserve this creation, guarding it from destruction. As for me, I will take on the role of the destroyer, completing the cosmic cycle."

Vishnu and BrahmaDev bowed in reverence, enlightened by the truth of their existence. Shiva, gazing upon them with compassion, said, "Now, I will grant you each a boon."

BrahmaDev, still clouded by pride, requested, "I wish for you to be born as my son." Vishnu, with humility, asked, "Let me always have the opportunity to serve you."

Shiva smiled, both pleased and stern. "BrahmaDev, I will fulfill your wish, but as a consequence of your pride, I curse you: you shall not be worshipped by anyone. Vishnu, your boon is gladly granted. You shall serve me, and in doing so, you will preserve the balance of creation."

2

SHIVA'S ATTIRE

Shiva, the Supreme Lord, is revered as *Trinetra* or *Triambaka*, the one with three eyes. His third eye, positioned vertically on his forehead, grants him the name *Phalanetra*. This third eye is not just a symbol; it embodies immense power, capable of incinerating anything in its gaze, which is why Shiva is also called *Agnimaya*, the one who wields fire.

Armed with his mighty trident, Shiva is known as *Trishuli*, and the trident itself is called *Pinakam*, giving him the name *Pinakapani*. His loyal companion, Nandi the bull, serves as his vehicle, and the sound of his *Damaru*, a small drum attached to his trident, echoes through the cosmos. It produces the primordial vibrations, the rhythm of creation and destruction, as Shiva performs his cosmic dance, *Tandava*.

On his head, Shiva holds both the crescent moon and the sacred river Ganga, flowing from the heavens. For this, he is known as *Chandrachooda* and *Gangadhara*. The moon represents the cycles of time, while the Ganga signifies the flow of life and purification.

Shiva, in his infinite wisdom and humility, often takes on the guise of a wandering ascetic, mingling with ordinary mortals unnoticed. On one such occasion, he roamed the forests where the great *Rishis* and their wives lived. Dressed as a vagabond, Shiva's divine presence went unrecognized by the sages, but their wives, captivated by his beauty and mysterious charm, were drawn to him. They did not realize that this wanderer was none other than Lord Shiva himself, the embodiment of all creation.

The Rishis, unsettled by their wives' sudden infatuation with the stranger, devised a plan to rid the forest of him. They tamed a ferocious, saber-toothed predator and set it loose, hoping it would slay the mysterious figure. But they were unaware that they had set their trap for the almighty himself. Shiva, with effortless grace, subdued the beast with his bare hands, and draped its skin over himself as a garment, a symbol of his triumph.

Undeterred, the Rishis conspired again, capturing venomous serpents from the wild and releasing them where Shiva lay resting. But when Shiva awoke, he calmly took the snakes and wrapped them around his neck and arms, transforming them into his adornments. His divine form, now adorned with the skins of beasts and the coiling serpents, radiated an otherworldly power, a testament to his transcendence over all fears and threats.

Realizing their folly, the Rishis abandoned their attempts to harm Shiva. Days passed, and Shiva, having walked unnoticed among the mortals, shed his human guise and returned to his celestial abode.

3

SAMUDRA MANTHAN

Maharshi Durvasa was once conducting a *Yajna* in Devalok, attended by many dignitaries, including IndraDev. Sage Durvasa offered Indra a special garland that had been given to him by Lord Shiva. Indra gladly accepted the gift, but as he returned, he carelessly placed the sacred garland on the trunk of his elephant, Airavat. Airavat, in a playful mood, tossed the garland to the ground and trampled it repeatedly, until it was utterly destroyed.

When Durvasa learned of this, he stormed towards Indra. Known for his fiery temper, Maharshi Durvasa was enraged by Indra's disregard for the garland, a sacred symbol of divinity that was meant to be treated as a spiritual offering. In his wrath, Durvasa cursed Indra: "You have not only insulted my gift by allowing its destruction, but you have also disrespected Lord Shiva's divine garland. I curse you, Indra! All the Devas, including you, will lose your divine powers and be reduced to mere mortals. You shall age, weaken, and eventually die of infirmity."

Devastated, IndraDev pleaded, "O revered Rishi, I admit my carelessness in placing the garland on Airavat's trunk. But I had no intention of disrespecting you or the almighty Lord Shiva. Airavat was beyond my control when it destroyed the garland. I tried my best to prevent it. Please, Maharshi, your curse will bring ruin upon the Devas. Without our powers, the Asuras will overrun us and take control of the world. Please, have mercy and neutralize the curse."

Durvasa, still fuming, replied, "IndraDev, your arrogance is known throughout the world. It may have been that arrogance which guided my curse. Sadly, a curse, once given, cannot be taken back. However, there is a way for you to regain your divine powers - by drinking the Amrit. To obtain it, you must churn the *Ksheera Sagara*."

The curse took immediate effect. The eternally youthful Devas began to age, their skin wrinkled, and their hair turned white. Their divine powers depleted rapidly, and in the battle that followed, the Asuras easily defeated the weakened Devas, seizing control of the universe. Helpless, the Devas turned to Lord Vishnu for aid.

Lord Vishnu said, "It is true that the Asuras now hold the upper hand. The Devas are wounded and demoralized. At this moment, I see no easy solution."

IndraDev responded, "Maharshi Durvasa told me about the Amrit, which holds undying power and is hidden within the Ksheera Sagara. But the Devas are too weak to churn the ocean on our own."

Lord Vishnu advised, "We can enlist the help of the Asuras. They too desire the Amrit. Approach them diplomatically and offer to share it once it is obtained. But do not worry - I will find a way to ensure they do not gain the nectar."

Following this plan, the Devas formed an uneasy alliance with the Asuras to churn the ocean for the nectar of immortality. The churning of Ksheera Sagara was a monumental task. Mount Mandara was used as the churning rod, and Vasuki, the king of serpents, became the churning rope. The Asuras, in their pride, insisted on holding Vasuki's head, while the Devas, following Vishnu's advice, held the tail. Those holding the head, including the Asuras, suffered from the venomous fumes Vasuki emitted.

As the Devas and Asuras pulled Vasuki's body alternately, the mountain began to rotate, churning the Ocean of Milk. But disaster struck when Mount Mandara began to sink into the ocean. Both the Devas and the Asuras tried to stop it but were dragged down along with the mountain. Desperate, the Devas cried for help.

It was then that Lord Vishnu took on a new form. Ages had passed since his first avatar, *Matsya*, saved the world from destruction. Now, it was time for his second avatar. Vishnu appeared as *Kurma*, the giant turtle, and supported the mountain on his back, ensuring the churning staff would not sink into the cosmic waters.

The *Samudra Manthan* (churning of the ocean) brought forth many divine treasures. From the depths of Ksheera Sagara emerged Goddess Lakshmi, who became the consort of Lord Vishnu. Countless jewels, Apsaras, and divine entities such as Kamadhenu, the wish-fulfilling cow, and Kalpavriksha, the wish-granting tree, also rose from the ocean. The divine horse Uchhaishravas, the Kaustubha gem, and the ever-blooming Parijat tree appeared as well, all of which were shared between the Devas and Asuras.

However, along with the treasures came a deadly byproduct: the lethal poison *Halahala*. The noxious fumes began to suffocate both the Devas and the Asuras. Realizing that if the poison was not contained, the entire universe would be doomed, they rushed to Brahma for guidance. Brahma advised them that only Lord Shiva could save them.

The Devas and Asuras approached Lord Shiva, pleading, "O Almighty, save us. The future of the universe depends on your mercy. Rescue us from the deadly toxin, Halahala."

Seeing no other option, Shiva made the ultimate sacrifice. He consumed the Halahala, holding the poison in his throat to prevent it from spreading. The sheer potency of the toxin turned Shiva's throat blue, earning him the name *Neelakanta*. Shiva's immense strength allowed him to endure the poison without harm, saving the universe from certain destruction.

Finally, Dhanvantari, the heavenly physician, emerged from the ocean with a pot of Amrit. But no sooner had the Amrit appeared than the alliance between the Devas and Asuras collapsed. A fierce battle erupted as both sides fought for the nectar of immortality. Overwhelmed, the Devas watched as the Asuras seized the Amrit and fled.

Once again, they appealed to Lord Vishnu for help. Vishnu, calm as ever, replied, "Do not worry. They will not taste a single drop of it."

Using his power of *Maya*, Vishnu assumed the form of Mohini, an enchanting damsel of unparalleled beauty. When Mohini approached the

Asuras, they were mesmerized and eagerly asked her to be their consort.

"How can I marry all of you?" Mohini replied playfully. "But I will choose one, if you can pass a test."

Intrigued, the Asuras asked, "What is the test?"

"I want all of you to close your eyes," she said. "Whoever keeps their eyes closed the longest shall be my husband."

Enthralled by her beauty, the Asuras complied. While their eyes were shut, Mohini took the pot of Amrit and returned to the Devas, distributing the nectar among them. As the Devas drank the Amrit, their youth and strength were restored, their powers renewed.

When one impatient Asura opened his eyes, he realized what had happened. "We've been tricked!" he cried, rousing the others. Furious, the Asuras charged at the Devas, but this time the Devas were invincible. A fierce battle ensued, and the Asuras were ultimately defeated. The Devas regained their dominion over Devalok, while the Asuras retreated to Patala, their hopes of immortality shattered.

4

SHIVA AND SATI

Once upon a time, Lord Shiva was deep in meditation. As the greatest Yogi in the world, his meditative state meant complete absorption, causing him to forget the world around him. All of his senses and power were focused solely on his meditation. This created a significant problem, as there was no one to carry out the divine duty of destruction. Consequently, the balance of Srishti (creation), Stiti (preservation), and Samhara (destruction) was disrupted.

BrahmaDev, the creator, was disturbed by this imbalance. He saw beings with sins living on without the process of

destruction, and he decided to take action to restore order. BrahmaDev, accompanied by his son KamaDev, the God of Love, approached Lord Shiva in his meditation.

BrahmaDev said to KamaDev, "Son, do you see how Lord Shiva has been meditating for ages? This is concerning. We must wake him up. You must find a way to end this eternal meditation."

KamaDev replied, "Father, I will carry out this task as if it's my life's purpose. But I need your help. Please create a beautiful girl and I will handle the rest."

BrahmaDev created Vasanth, the embodiment of spring, and Malayanil, the breeze, who became KamaDev's assistants. Together, they did everything they could to wake Lord Shiva, but all their efforts were in vain. BrahmaDev became despondent. From his deep sigh, the air transformed into arrows, which he handed to KamaDev, instructing him to use them as weapons of love to awaken Shiva. KamaDev, armed with these new arrows, approached Lord Shiva and began shooting them one by one. Yet, nothing happened. Defeated, KamaDev returned to BrahmaDev and apologized for his failure.

Seeing that all efforts had failed, a distressed BrahmaDev began to pray to Lord Vishnu. At that very moment, Vishnu appeared before him and said, "BrahmaDev! What is the cause of your grief? Why are you so troubled? I will take care of it."

BrahmaDev replied, "Oh Vishnu, Lord Shiva is in deep meditation and unaware of what is happening in the world. The only way to wake him is to make him fall in love with someone. I have tried, with the help of my son, but our efforts have been fruitless. That is why I am so unhappy. I would be grateful if you could help me succeed."

Vishnu smiled and said, "Dear BrahmaDev, there is only one way to achieve this. Pray to Devi ParaSakti. She will incarnate as the daughter of Daksha on Earth and will marry Lord Shiva. But this will not happen easily. You must convince Daksha to meditate and ask for Devi ParaSakti as his daughter." After saying this, Vishnu disappeared.

Satisfied with Vishnu's advice, BrahmaDev went to visit Daksha. Appearing before Emperor Daksha, BrahmaDev said, "Son Daksha, you must perform penance to please Devi ParaSakti so that she will be born as your daughter." Without hesitation, Daksha and his wife began meditating with the hope of receiving Devi ParaSakti's blessings. After three thousand years of meditation, Devi ParaSakti appeared before them.

Daksha said, "Mother of the Universe, grant us a wish."

Devi ParaSakti replied, "Daksha, I am pleased with your prayers. Ask for whatever you wish and I will grant it."

Daksha humbly requested, "Great Devi, Lord Shiva remains without a wife, which is essential for maintaining the balance of the universe. I humbly ask that you be born as my daughter and marry Lord Shiva, for the sake of the gods and all beings."

Devi ParaSakti agreed, but added a condition. "I will be born as your daughter and marry Shiva, but if I ever feel disrespected by you, I will leave my mortal body and return to Parabrahma. You must always remember this." With this, Devi ParaSakti blessed Daksha and disappeared. Soon after, Daksha and his wife were blessed with a daughter, whom they named Sati.

Years later, BrahmaDev and Narada visited Daksha's palace to see Sati. BrahmaDev raised her up with affection and said, "Dear Sati, your secret wish will come true. Lord Shiva will be your husband. There is no need to worry." Delighted by this news, both Daksha and Sati rejoiced.

As Sati grew older, she became a devoted follower of Lord Shiva. One day, she told her mother, "Mother, I wish to meditate to win Lord Shiva's favour and become his wife. Please give me your blessing." Her mother consented, recognizing Shiva as the ideal husband for her daughter.

Sati left the comforts of the palace and began her meditation. Day and night, she worshipped Lord Shiva with unwavering focus. Her devotion reached Lord Shiva, gradually waking him from his deep meditation. When the Devas saw this, they gathered at Mount Kailas to meet him.

"Namaste, Lord Mahadeva!" they greeted him.

Shiva opened his eyes to see Lord Vishnu, BrahmaDev, and thousands of other gods. "What brings you all here?" Shiva asked.

BrahmaDev replied, "Lord, we came to remind you of an important matter. As I create and Vishnu preserves, the number of Asuras has increased, and their sins are rampant. You are the only one who can restore balance. However, you need a companion, just as we have. For the sake of universal balance, you should marry."

Shiva smiled and said, "You two are dear to me. I will marry, but only if my wife supports my ideals. If she hinders them in any way, our union will end."

BrahmaDev joyfully replied, "We have already found the perfect bride for you. She is the incarnation of Devi ParaSakti and is named Sati. She is meditating to be your wife. Please bless her and make her your consort."

Shiva agreed and went to see Sati. Her devotion pleased him greatly, and he appeared before her. Overwhelmed by his divine presence, Sati expressed her wish to be his wife. Shiva, also wishing the same, blessed her and disappeared.

Sati returned to the palace and shared the joyful news with her mother. Meanwhile, Shiva informed BrahmaDev of his decision to marry Sati.

Overjoyed, BrahmaDev went to Daksha and said, "Daksha, your daughter's wish has come true. Lord Shiva has agreed to marry Sati. How do you feel about this?"

Daksha replied, "It is an honour beyond words. I will make all the necessary arrangements for the wedding."

The marriage of Lord Shiva and Sati was soon arranged, and gods and celestial beings from all over the universe gathered to witness the union. On the auspicious day, Lord Shiva entered Daksha's palace with BrahmaDev, Vishnu, and the Devas by his side. Daksha welcomed Lord Shiva with great joy and organized the ceremony with gifts and feasts for all.

Shiva, pleased with the arrangements, said to BrahmaDev, "I am grateful for everything. Ask for anything, and I will grant your wish."

BrahmaDev replied, "Lord Shiva, I wish to establish a temple where people from all over the world can come to pray to you and have their sins cleansed."

Shiva granted his wish, and the temple was established. With the entire celestial realm in attendance, Lord Shiva and Sati were married, marking a new chapter in the divine history of the gods.

5

THE DAKSHA YAGA

Durvasa Rishi is one of the most feared and revered sages of ancient times. He was so perfect in prayers and meditations that he had God-like powers at his disposal. Rishi Durvasa's curses and blessings have immediate effects. One day, Devi Jagatambika became very pleased with Durvasa's worship and gifted him a garland made from her own body. Thereafter, Durvasa visited the castle of Daksha while wearing this garland. Seeing this beautiful, shining garland, Daksha expressed his fascination with it and told Durvasa that he wished to own it. Rishi Durvasa is known for his moods. He is the kind of person who gifts when he feels happy and curses

when he is annoyed. However, for Daksha's luck, Durvasa was somehow happy at that moment and gave him the garland without hesitation. With extreme delight, Daksha took the garland and placed it inside his bedroom. The bedroom of a common man cannot hold the chastity of a sage's chamber. Furthermore, Daksha engaged in intimate and passionate activities with his wife while the sacred garland was inside his bedroom. Thus, Daksha's act was an insult to the holy garland. Lord Shiva learned of this incident and appeared before Daksha, scolding him without hesitation. Humiliated by Lord Shiva, Daksha became angry and swore revenge against him.

Later, several sages decided to conduct a grand Yajna. They selected a place called Prayaga as the venue for this splendid ceremony. Many important dignitaries, including BrahmaDev, Sanatanists, scholars, Devas, kings, and Pundits, gathered to take part in the event. Various competitions and debates were conducted at the same venue, most related to science, philosophy, mathematics, art, dance, and music.

Lord Shiva arrived with his wife, Sati. Everyone stood up in respect for the Lord of All and then sat back, discussing how lucky they were to have Lord Shiva among them. At that time, unexpectedly, Daksha also arrived. Everyone approached him to show gratitude and respect, while Lord Shiva remained seated. He considered Daksha an egoist who took pride in owning all the luck and fortune without deserving it. Seeing that Lord Shiva remained immobile, Daksha felt anger.

"Look at his arrogance. He claims to be a great person. In reality, he always associates with ghosts and demons while residing in a graveyard. Yet, such a low-life shows no respect towards me. This is *Adharma*. Anyone who walks, talks, sits, or befriends him will become a sinner. Shiva, I curse you. From this day onwards, you will be expelled from all four castes. You will become terribly ugly and will not have a proper life." As soon as Daksha finished his atrocious words, all the sages present agreed with him. They misunderstood Shiva as a cruel being. The Devas joined Daksha's newly formed gang and began insulting Shiva. But Lord Shiva sat there silently, witnessing this humongous slander without replying.

However, Nandi, the trusted associate of Lord Shiva, who was a spectator to the insult from Daksha and others towards Shiva, became furious. His eyes turned red. He shouted, "How dare you fools insult the one who balances creation, protection, and destruction? What quality do you possess to offend my master? You are attacking the one who is the main cause of this Yajna's success. How dare you make fun of him?"

Hearing Nandi's words, rage blinded Daksha, and he became uncontrollable. He again began to insult and curse Shiva. Nandi replied with equal force, cursing all Brahmins, including Daksha, out of resentment towards him. Lord Shiva smiled, seeing Nandi's aggression towards Daksha. He calmed Nandi and said, "Hey Nandi, you are a scholar. Therefore, aggression is not the appropriate behavior for you. You have just cursed all these Brahmins because of a slight misunderstanding. Keep in mind that no matter who curses us, nothing will affect us. Daksha's curse will never harm us. Trust me; just keep calm and relax." Nandi regained his composure upon witnessing Shiva's attitude. After a while, Lord Shiva and Nandi returned to Kailas.

Outraged, Daksha returned to his castle. He spent most of his time planning revenge against Shiva. He even began to insult those who prayed to Lord Shiva. Thus, he became an arch-enemy of the God Almighty. Consequently, he decided to conduct a grand Yaga and swore not to invite Shiva and Sati.

Back at Mt. Kailas, Sati was conversing with her friends in one of the valleys. At that time, she saw Chandra with her sister Rohini passing by. Sati wanted to know where her sister was going.

She asked her favorite companion, Vijaya, "Dear Vijaya! I saw my sister Rohini dressed beautifully, walking with her husband Chandra. Usually, she tells me before going anywhere. I don't know why she didn't do that today. Is something special happening at home? It is highly unlikely for something like that to occur without my knowledge. Anyway, can you ask her where she is heading?"

After listening to Sati, Vijaya went to Chandra and asked, "ChandraDev! Sati Devi told me to ask you where you and Rohini Devi are going."

"What? Sati doesn't know about it? Her father, Daksha, is conducting a grand Yaga. Many festivities are being thrown around there related to this Yaga. He called everyone to attend it. We are going there to participate. I wonder why he didn't invite Sati." Vijaya became confused hearing this. Without replying, she ran back to Sati and said, "Devi Sati, your father has committed a terrible offence."

"Offence? What offence? I don't understand," she asked desperately.

Vijaya replied, "Your father is hosting a grand Yaga with much celebration. Every single being in this world is aware of this occasion except you. He invited everyone to attend as well. They are all going there. It is a dreadful wrong that your father didn't invite you."

Sati was shocked hearing Vijaya's words. She thought for a minute, "Why didn't my father inform me about hosting a big Yaga? Why did he ignore me and my husband while inviting all the Devas and sages?" She became depressed and went to Lord Shiva.

Seeing his wife approach with a sorrowful air, Lord Shiva asked, "Dear, what happened to you? You look so depressed and disappointed. What is the cause of your unhappiness?"

Sati replied with a sigh, "I learned that my father is hosting a grand Yaga at this very moment. Everyone, including Devas, rishis, and even your associates BrahmaDev and Vishnu, are attending this celebration. But he didn't invite us. My sister has already gone there. This is really heartbreaking. I don't know why he ignored us while inviting everyone else."

Lord Shiva spoke in a calm voice, "Dear SatiDevi, you should rid yourself of the desire to attend this Yaga right now."

"No, we should go there no matter what," Sati replied.

"Sati, it is wrong to attend an uninvited event," Shiva said.

"Why didn't he call us? He did this on purpose."

"Sati, your father has been troubling me with his arrows of evil words. Those who are attending your father's Yaga are egomaniacs and nitwits. They are all proud of themselves while knowing nothing about the Yaga's sole purpose. If we go, we will become targets for Daksha's insults in front of all those people. It is better to die than suffer such humiliation. Therefore, we must not go."

Sati replied, "How can the Yaga succeed without the presence of you, the God of All? My father is cruel. I must know why he didn't invite you. I should also find out the opinions of those who gathered there. Therefore, you should let me go. I don't think an invitation is necessary for a daughter to attend her father's Yaga."

After hearing what Sati had to say, Shiva replied, "Devi! I'm not stopping you if you wish to go there desperately. I already said what I have to say. You are free to do whatever you want. However, you shouldn't go alone; take Nandi with you. Make sure you look like a queen when you attend the ceremony, and don't go empty-handed; take some gifts for your father."

Sati felt happy after Shiva allowed her to attend the Yaga. Thus,

Sati dressed in jewels and silk clothes and departed for the Yaga.

Accompanied by the Shivaganas, Sati arrived at Daksha's royal palace, where the grand Yaga was in progress. She observed the ceremony from the entrance of the palace itself. The venue was crowded with Devas, Asuras, kings, ministers, diplomats, and Gandharvas. It was luxuriously decorated with vibrant materials. Sati felt perplexed by the scene before her. Slowly, she walked toward the Yaga venue.

Veerani, Sati's mother, noticed her arrival, and the smile on her face suddenly vanished. She couldn't bear to witness the insult her husband was showing towards their own daughter. Veerani wept as she realized that her daughter had come to the ceremony despite not being invited. She ran towards Sati and took her by the hand, leading her to the main venue. However, Daksha, witnessing this scene, was not pleased at all. He completely ignored Sati, refusing even to look at her. The Devas present at the event showed no acknowledgment of Sati. They merely murmured to each other while casting disgusted glances in her direction. Daksha shot a fierce glare at Veerani, and she immediately released Sati's hand.

Determined, Sati approached her father and touched his feet out of respect. Yet, Daksha did not look at her or utter a single word. Sati found it difficult to understand her father's behavior and stood alone, her eyes filled with tears as she observed the Yaga.

On one side of the venue, luxurious offerings were reserved for dignitaries like Vishnu, BrahmaDev, and IndraDev, but there were no offerings for Lord Shiva. Sati could no longer endure her distress. Anger welled up within her, and she decided to confront her father about this grave insult. Although she did not mind her father's behavior toward her, she could not fathom his disrespect toward her beloved husband.

Taking center stage at the venue, she shouted, "Father, aren't you aware that Lord Shiva is the symbol of auspiciousness and the only person who can ensure the success of a Yaga? He maintains the balance of the entire universe, which consists of living beings of all shapes and sizes. With his mere presence, he can bring bliss to any Yajna. How dare you ignore the Almighty Lord Shiva? You are a fool, a brute, and a sinner. I am ashamed to call you my father. You have made yourself despicable by insulting Lord Shiva!"

Turning her raging eyes to Vishnu and BrahmaDev, she continued, "You fools, how could you participate in this Yaga, accepting the invitation of this tyrant? You have completely failed to understand Lord Shiva." Embarrassed by Sati's words, all the Devas, including Vishnu and BrahmaDev, felt ashamed and guilty. Meanwhile, the furious Daksha became angrier than ever and rushed toward Sati.

Daksha roared, "Sati, you relentless, egoistic fool! How dare you speak such atrocities? You are no longer my daughter. You do not deserve to attend this Yaga, as you are the wife of a barbarian. Why did you come here without an invitation? Leave at once if you have any dignity left. You will gain nothing by boasting here. It is better that you leave on your own; otherwise, I will be forced to kick you out. Those present here know your husband well. He is no God; he is just a filthy savage who associates with zombies. His very presence will pollute this divine Yaga. I cannot allow that to happen, and that is why I did not invite him. As his wife, you are also tainted by your association with him. Therefore, you should not be here either."

The participants of the Yaga fell silent, becoming spectators of this bizarre event as Daksha continued, "Does he possess any wisdom? He is a fool and a sinner. I made a terrible mistake by allowing you to marry him. I regret that decision deeply. Sati, stay away from this Yaga right now. No one here is interested in your drama."

Daksha's derogatory words made Sati furious. Bitterly glaring at her father, she thought, "How can I face my husband after enduring such insults? He told me not to attend this ceremony uninvited. This is the dire consequence of ignoring his advice. He will definitely ask about the Yaga, and how can I tell him

about the outrage that occurred here? It is better if I do not return."

Sati shouted, "You are all sinners! Do not think that my father is the only one responsible for this grave insult toward Lord Shiva. All of you who remained silent in the face of this blasphemy will face dreadful consequences. You may continue to abuse my Lord for your own comfort, but I can no longer endure this!"

As soon as she finished speaking, she leaped into the grand ritual fire. Within minutes, Sati was reduced to ashes. The Devas, witnessing these horrifying events, panicked. They had never anticipated such a gruesome incident. Subsequently, they began blaming Daksha, shouting, "Murderer! Tyrant! Crude!" and so on.

The Shivaganas who had accompanied Sati lost all composure and began attacking the authorities of the Yaga, including Daksha. Daksha's warriors fought back, and some of the despondent Shivaganas threw themselves into the Yaga fire. The entire venue erupted into chaos. Vishnu and BrahmaDev panicked at the sight, unable to find a way to stop the mayhem. All the Devas and other dignitaries fled the scene, startled and anxious. The surviving Shivaganas retreated to Mt. Kailas.

Lord Shiva, who was meditating at that moment, opened his

eyes to the desperate calls of the Shivaganas at his feet. He sensed that something was wrong, as the Yaga should not have concluded this early, and most of the Shivaganas, along with Sati, were missing. He asked, "What happened? Where are the others? Where is Sati?"

One of the Shivaganas replied dismally, "Lord, the cruel Daksha affronted Devi Sati in front of all the dignitaries at the Yaga and spoke disgraceful things about you as well. An enraged Sati shouted at her father in response. Daksha continued to insult her, hurling insults at you."

Lord Shiva inquired, "Then, where is she?"

A disheartened Shivagana responded, "The weight of the insults drove Sati to self-immolate in the Yaga fire. Some of our companions jumped into the fire out of desperation, while others tried to attack Daksha and were killed by his warriors. We had no other option but to inform you about this dreadful situation. My Lord, please forgive us. Daksha's arrogance must come to an end."

Blazing with rage, Lord Shiva lost his serenity and transformed into his transcendent form of wrath - Rudra. As Rudra, Lord Shiva, who oversees the divine duty of destruction, could obliterate the entire world with a single stroke. His third eye opened, emitting a burning radiance. From the inferno emerged the incredible Virabhadra, accompanied by the deafening sound of thunder and the blaze of a thousand lightning strikes. Immediately, Lord Shiva appointed him as the chief of the Shivaganas.

Virabhadra stood taller than a giant, possessing a thousand arms and exuding an intimidating presence, like a flaming volcano. After saluting Lord Shiva, he asked, "Master! The sole purpose of my existence is to execute your orders. Whether it is to crush mountains or drain oceans, no one can defeat me in battle. Please bless me and command me, my Lord."

Lord Shiva replied, "I created you for an imperative mission.

Daksha, the son of BrahmaDev, is a brutal tyrant who has frequently humiliated me throughout the ages. Although I am not affected by it, my wife Sati ended her life in the Yaga fire due to his abuses. We cannot remain passive. The Yaga is still ongoing, and it must not be allowed to conclude. Go to Daksha's palace, stop the Yaga from continuing, and annihilate Daksha and his sycophants!"

Without wasting any time, Virabhadra set off for Daksha's Yaga, accompanied by a battalion of a million Shivaganas. Meanwhile, at the venue of the Yaga, Daksha and the others felt the earth tremble. Initially, they thought it was an earthquake, but soon they saw the vicious force of the Shivaganas approaching, led by a gigantic figure with a thousand arms. The participants of the Daksha Yaga panicked, and Daksha, alarmed, was at a loss for what to do.

Daksha took his wife and prayed to Lord Vishnu, saying, "Dear Lord, I conducted this Yaga in belief of your supreme power. Please protect me from these demons. Only you have the power to help me."

Vishnu replied, "You have caused this, Daksha. Your arrogance has led to your downfall. I may be able to help the Yaga continue, but no one can assist you except Lord Shiva himself. If I attempt to protect you, I fear I will be harmed as well. Plead with Lord Shiva and hope he forgives you."

By the time Vishnu was speaking, the army of Shivaganas had already begun their assault on the Yaga ground. A ferocious battle erupted between the Devas and the Shivaganas, turning the Yaga into a field of carnage. Some of the Devas fled, while others, under the leadership of IndraDev, fought fiercely. However, they were forced to retreat when they realized that they would surely fail in the battle.

Virabhadra, along with his army of Shivaganas, entered the Yaga platform to stop the Rishis from continuing their rituals. The Rishis prayed to Vishnu for assistance. Lord Vishnu leaped onto the platform and confronted Virabhadra, saying, "The Yaga must

continue. I swore to protect it. Virabhadra! You don't know who I am. I'm a servant of Lord Shiva. Therefore, you mustn't see me as an enemy of Lord Shiva. I attended this Yaga and swore to protect it at the behest of the ignorant Daksha. I am duty-bound to protect his Yaga. You must get through me if you want to stop it."

Virabhadra replied, "I am pleased to hear that you are a servant of my master as well. However, I am bound to my mission." The clash between Virabhadra and Vishnu continued. Vishnu deployed all his weapons, including the Sudarsana Chakra, but they were all neutralized by Virabhadra. Realizing that the confrontation would not end favorably for him, Vishnu retreated and vanished into thin air.

The remaining Devas and others at the venue recognized their mistakes and fled after praying to Lord Shiva. The Rishis conducting the Yaga were brutally assaulted by the Shivaganas. Ultimately, the Yaga came to a disastrous end. A terror-stricken Daksha hid under the platform. Seeing this, Virabhadra grabbed Daksha by his legs and hurled him over the Yaga platform. He then decapitated Daksha and tossed his head into the Yaga fire. With a victorious laugh, Virabhadra returned to Mount Kailas.

Virabhadra informed Lord Shiva about the bloodshed. Although Lord Shiva was pleased with the outcome, he still mourned the loss of his wife. Just then, all the Devas who participated in the Daksha Yaga, along with Lord Vishnu and BrahmaDev, arrived at Mount Kailas. They immediately bowed to him and asked for forgiveness. "We acknowledge our mistakes. Daksha was an ignorant fool, and we fell for his words. We failed to understand you. Lord Shiva, you are the God of all; you are the supreme God.

Please forgive us."

Lord Shiva replied, "I accept your apologies. But remember, what happened was caused by the actions of Daksha."

The guests said, "Dear Lord Shiva, we have a request. Please bring back all those who lost their lives at the hands of the Shivaganas, including Daksha. Only you have the power and the compassion to do so. We are at your feet."

Accompanied by Virabhadra, Lord Shiva visited the site of the Daksha Yaga, where he saw thousands of dead bodies. He announced, "I will restore life to all those who lie dead here." And thus, all the Devas and Rishis breathed life again and began to pray to Lord Shiva. However, Daksha's head had been burned beyond recovery by the Yaga flames. Lord Shiva commanded, "Place a goat's head on Daksha's body so that he may live again." Once this was done, Daksha came back to life. He immediately bowed to Lord Shiva and said, "Dear Lord, even after I have abused you and caused you immense pain, you have still blessed me. I do not know how to thank you. I will be your servant for the rest of my life."

With Lord Shiva's blessings, all the Rishis and Devas were overjoyed. Although Sati had turned to ashes due to her act of self-immolation, she, who forsook her body, would eventually reunite with Lord Shiva as his spouse once again.

6

THE BIRTH OF MARS

After the demise of Sati, Lord Shiva entered a deep meditation on Mount Kailas. Years and Yugas passed, and the power of his meditation grew stronger and stronger. The intensity of his meditation was so great that it required tremendous effort to awaken from it, causing beads of sweat to form on his forehead.

One of these drops of sweat fell to Earth. When Shiva's sweat touched the surface, a miraculous event occurred: a baby was born. The child had reddish skin and radiated a divine aura. Like any newborn, the baby began to cry. This cry was heard by Bhoomi Devi, the goddess of Earth.

Taking the form of a woman, Bhoomi Devi came to Kailas to meet Lord Shiva. Upon seeing the divine child, she took him in her arms and comforted him, successfully soothing his cries. She kissed the child, bathed him, and fed him her breast milk, becoming his mother through this nurturing act. Sensing this, Lord Shiva was filled with joy.

Shiva said, "Bhoomi, you are truly compassionate. By caring for the child born from me and nursing him, you have become his mother. Take this baby and raise him as your own. Though this divine child was born from my sweat, he will be known by your name. He will be a generous being and will bring prosperity to many."

Bhoomi Devi replied, "Dear Lord, I am deeply honored by your blessing. I could not ask for anything more. This is like a dream come true. I will raise this divine child as if he were born from my own womb."

With Lord Shiva's blessing, Bhoomi Devi left Mount Kailas with the baby. She raised him with great care, treating him as her most precious treasure. His presence brought her immense joy and contentment. The boy became known as Bhauma.

Upon reaching adulthood, Bhauma went to Kashi and performed an intense penance to please Lord Shiva. After years of devotion, Lord Shiva appeared before him and blessed him. "Dear Bhauma," Shiva announced, "you are as radiant and glorious as any celestial body. Therefore, you shall ascend to the status of a planet. From now on, you will reside in the heavens and shine as a celestial being."

Thus, Bhauma was established in the solar system as the planet Mars, known as Mangala.

There is another version of this story that tells a slightly different tale. In this version, instead of sweat, Lord Shiva emitted immense heat while in his deep trance. The heat intensified, and at its peak, a beam of energy struck the Earth, giving birth to the child.

Lord Shiva named the baby Khuja, and like in the previous story, Bhoomi Devi raised him as her own. Khuja later ascended to the ranks of celestial beings and became known as Mangala, the planet Mars. Khuja is also renowned as the god of iron.

7

RISE OF TARAKASURA

Maharshi Kashyapa was the son of Marichi, whose father was BrahmaDev. Kashyapa was married to thirteen daughters of Daksha. Among his wives, Diti, the eldest, gave birth to two sons, Hiranyaksha and Hiranyakashipu. Both were Asuras, and they terrorized mortals and heavenly beings alike. For their vicious acts, both were slain by avatars of Lord Vishnu at the request of the Devas.

Grieving the loss of her two sons, Diti began an intense meditation, seeking to give birth to a son powerful enough to rival the Devas, including Indra. However, when her meditation reached its final stage, IndraDev sabotaged it, preventing Diti from birthing such a powerful offspring.

Determined to fulfill her desire for vengeance, Diti, after receiving Kashyapa's blessings, resumed her meditation, which lasted for ten thousand years, fueled by her hatred for Indra and the other Devas. As a result, she gave birth to a son who was powerful and fearless. He was named Vajranga.

Vajranga mastered the Vedas, martial arts, and various sciences. One day, after years of intense training, he asked his mother, "Mother, what would you like me to do now?"

Diti replied, "Son, neutralize IndraDev, who killed your brothers."

Without hesitation, Vajranga stormed into Devalok, singlehandedly defeating Indra's warriors. After winning the battle, he grabbed Indra by the hair, dragged him, and dropped him at Diti's feet. Upon learning of these events, BrahmaDev, at Kashyapa's request, appeared before Vajranga and asked him to spare Indra's life.

Vajranga loosened his grip on Indra and said, "Indra is a tyrant. He killed my brothers, and I was only fulfilling my mother's wishes. Now that Indra has faced what he deserves, he may return to heaven and continue his reign. I have no desire to conquer anything. Now that my duty is done, I wish to lead a peaceful life. Please, BrahmaDev, guide me."

Pleased with Vajranga's words, BrahmaDev replied, "Dear Vajranga, I will bless you with a wife named Varangi. Live a happy life with her."

Vajranga returned to his abode with Varangi, and they led a tranquil life, far from the pursuits of power and conquest. Their love for each other brought them immense happiness. One day, Vajranga, pleased by his wife's love and devotion, asked her, "Beloved, I am truly grateful to have you as my wife. You shower me with so much love. I am devoted to granting you whatever you desire. Please, tell me what you wish for."

Varangi replied, "If you are truly pleased with me, then I ask you to create a son who can conquer the three worlds."

Vajranga was shocked to hear this. Though he remained calm, he replied cautiously, "My dear, we should not see the Devas as our enemies. If I grant your wish, the balance of the three worlds will be disrupted. It will be a catastrophe for every being in the universe. Yet, I am bound to fulfill your wish, as I have given you my word."

Although hesitant, Vajranga began a deep meditation to acquire the power necessary to grant Varangi's desire. He meditated for over four thousand years. When he finally returned home, he found Varangi in deep despair and mourning.

"What has happened, my love?" he asked.

"It's better if I don't tell you," Varangi replied.

After his constant urging, she finally revealed the truth. "While you were away in meditation, that tyrant Indra invaded and tormented me relentlessly. I was on the verge of ending my life, but then you returned. Had you arrived any later, I would have been dead by now."

Furious, Vajranga thought, "Indra's arrogance has gone too far. I must take revenge. Though I have the power to destroy him, I will not, as I swore to BrahmaDev to live a peaceful life. But my son will carry out the retribution."

Soon after, Varangi gave birth to a boy. At the moment of his birth, bad omens such as earthquakes, volcanic eruptions, meteor strikes, and raging storms filled the earth. The child grew at an astonishing rate, faster than anyone could imagine. Word of the birth of this savior spread among the Asuras, and they flocked from all corners of the world to see their new protector. Maharshi Kashyapa immediately named the child "Taraka."

As Taraka reached adulthood, the Asuras declared him their

sovereign leader. The formidable Tarakasura addressed his subjects, saying, "My fellow Asuras, it is our sacred duty to bring prosperity to our kind. The Devas are our sworn enemies by creed. They have tormented us for generations. It is time to put an end to this. We must annihilate every Deva alive."

Determined to gain the power needed to conquer the three worlds, Tarakasura undertook an intense and prolonged meditation. For one hundred years, he stood on one leg, focusing on the sun. For the next hundred years, he balanced on a single toe. He survived on water alone for a hundred years and then lived on air for another century. Taraka spent a hundred years meditating in water and another hundred years in fire. Finally, for the last hundred years, he meditated while standing upside down, offering slices of his own flesh as a sacrifice. Upon completing his penance, Tarakasura became the most powerful Asura ever to exist.

BrahmaDev appeared before him and said, "Tarakasura, your penance is extraordinary. You may now ask for any boon you desire."

Tarakasura replied, "BrahmaDev, I harbor eternal hatred for the Devas. They have oppressed my kind for ages. My wish is this: make me so powerful that no one can ever kill me."

BrahmaDev, concerned by the request, responded, "My boy, no mortal can achieve immortality. However, I can grant you an exception: only one being will be able to kill you - a person you least expect."

Tarakasura paused to think. He knew that Lord Shiva, the great yogi, was unlikely to marry and have a child. Confident, he answered, "Very well. Let it be that only the son of Lord Shiva can kill me." BrahmaDev granted the boon and left.

Tarakasura went on to conquer everything except the heavens. Ruling the three worlds and tormenting the Devas had always been his ultimate goal. With an army of one hundred million soldiers and beasts, Taraka launched an invasion on Devalok.

The Devas, led by Indra, defended their realm, but the ensuing battle was devastating. The Devas suffered heavy losses, and those who survived fled in retreat.

Lord Vishnu arrived to aid in the defense of the Devas, but even his presence could not turn the tide. The Asuras unleashed a ferocious assault on Vishnu, and ultimately, the Devas faced a humiliating defeat. All the surviving Devas, including Vishnu, were taken prisoner by the Asuras. Tarakasura subjected them to various forms of torment, claiming the throne of the heavens and declaring himself the supreme ruler of the universe.

Hearing of these events, BrahmaDev appeared before Tarakasura and pleaded, "Tarakasura, remember that you are invincible because of the boon I granted you. I urge you to leave the heavens and release the Devas. You can continue to rule the universe from your own realm, where you will still enjoy every luxury."

Taraka replied, "I have achieved what my ancestors only dreamed of. I have the power to end the Deva race. Indra, their leader, is now at my mercy. He can rule as my vassal, but his life at my feet will be the ultimate torture for him."

Obeying BrahmaDev's request, Tarakasura returned to his castle on earth, ruling the three worlds as the supreme sovereign. While the Devas were allowed to return to the heavens, the Asuras maintained control over every corner of the universe.

Desperate for a solution, the Devas, along with Vishnu, approached BrahmaDev. They said, "We must find a way to defeat Tarakasura. He seems invincible, and his rule has plunged the universe into darkness."

BrahmaDev replied, "No one in the entire universe can defeat him - except one."

"Who is it?" the Devas asked in unison.

"The son of Lord Shiva," BrahmaDev answered.

8

SHIVA AND PARVATI

The merciless Tarakasura was terrorizing the entire universe. Each day, he conquered new territories and oppressed the inhabitants. The Devas, including the mighty Indra, tried repeatedly to defeat Tarakasura and his army, but all their efforts were in vain. After a deliberation, the Devas concluded that only a child of Lord Shiva could defeat Tarakasura.

However, following the demise of Sati, Lord Shiva had retreated into deep meditation. This concerned the Devas, especially BrahmaDev and Lord Vishnu. They feared that if Shiva remained in his meditation, he would never marry, and without a son, there would be no one to slay Tarakasura.

In response, the Devas, led by BrahmaDev and Vishnu, approached Himavat, the king of mountains.

"Dear Himavat, mighty king of the mountains, we have a most important task for you," BrahmaDev said.

Himavat, eager to serve, asked, "Please tell me what it is, and I will carry it out without fail."

Lord Vishnu replied, "You may be aware of Lord Shiva's current state. His wife, Devi Sati, forsook her body due to the insult of her father, Daksha. Lord Shiva is without a companion, and this is a grave situation. We need someone to marry him. Therefore, Himavat, you and your wife, Mena, must perform penance to please Devi ParaShakti. She will be born to you as a daughter on earth, and this daughter will marry Lord Shiva, bringing great celestial blessings."

Himavat asked, "But, my lord, Lord Shiva has vowed never to marry anyone except Sati. Will he truly marry my daughter?"

BrahmaDev replied, "Yes, he will. Sati was the incarnation of Devi ParaShakti, and she only disowned her mortal form during the Daksha Yaga. She will reincarnate as your daughter. Essentially, the daughter born to you will be none other than Sati herself, and Lord Shiva will recognize this and accept her."

Enchanted by this revelation, Himavat and Mena began their worship and penance towards Devi ParaShakti as soon as the Devas left. Their meditation lasted for ages, and eventually, Devi ParaShakti appeared before them. She granted them a boon, and they asked her to be born as their daughter. Devi ParaShakti agreed and disappeared.

Years passed, and though Himavat and Mena had many children, none of them were girls. Finally, Parvati was born, and they knew without a doubt that she was the incarnation of Devi

ParaShakti. In time, Parvati learned of her divine purpose - to become the wife of Lord Shiva. Determined, she set off to Mount Kailash to worship him and win his heart.

Unfortunately, Lord Shiva, deeply immersed in his meditation, did not notice Parvati, no matter how devotedly she worshipped him. Seeing her plight, Kama Dev, the God of Love, came to her aid. Kama Dev had the power to ignite passion in anyone at first sight by striking them with his arrow of desire.

Kama Dev shot his arrow at Lord Shiva, breaking his meditation. But instead of falling in love instantly, Shiva, enraged by the disturbance, opened his third eye and incinerated Kama Dev on the spot, reducing him to ashes.

However, upon seeing Parvati, Shiva was moved. He walked toward her and asked, "How can I help you?"

Parvati replied, "I have longed for you for ages. I wish for you to be my husband. But in my pursuit of this, the God of Love, Kama

Dev, met a tragic fate. Please, my lord, I beg you to bring him back to life."

Recognizing that Parvati was indeed the reincarnation of Sati, Shiva said, "Devi, I can restore Kama Dev to life. But as his body has been reduced to ashes, he will live without a physical form."

Thus, Kama Dev was revived as "Ananga" (the bodiless one) and existed as an invisible force of love from that moment onward.

However, Parvati had to continue her intense meditation and worship of Lord Shiva to achieve her goal. She settled near Mount Kailas with her companions and dedicated herself to her worship. Lord Shiva noticed her devotion but wanted to test her commitment to him.

One day, disguised as a wandering Brahmin, Lord Shiva arrived at Parvati's shelter. Parvati did not recognize him and assumed he was a poor wanderer. She welcomed him into her shelter and offered him food. The Brahmin asked, "Young lady, I am astonished to see such a beautiful girl undertaking meditation and worship that even great Rishis find difficult. What is your purpose? Whom are you trying to please?"

With a gentle smile, Parvati replied, "In my previous life, I was Sati, the wife of Lord Shiva. I left my body because of the disrespect my father, Daksha, showed towards Lord Shiva. It is my destiny to marry Shiva again in this life. I have no existence without him. For the welfare of the universe, I must marry him, and that is why I continue my meditation - to win his heart and become his wife."

The Brahmin laughed loudly, "You seem to know little about Shiva."

Curious, Parvati asked, "You know him?"

Still laughing, the Brahmin replied, "Yes, better than anyone else in the world. But I advise you to abandon your efforts. It's a complete waste of time. You'd be better off doing something else."

Puzzled, Parvati asked, "What do you mean? Please explain."

Ending his laughter, the Brahmin said, "This Shiva of yours is an emotionless, irresponsible being. He is a shameless wanderer who wears nothing but animal skins and covers himself in ashes. He has venomous snakes wrapped around his neck and limbs. His eyes are fierce, and he belongs to no caste or clan. He has no home and no known parents. He keeps company with ghosts and corpses. He is hideous to look at, with ten arms, and people avoid him out of fear. No wonder Daksha didn't invite him to the grand yajna! You're far too refined to seek a man like him. Why settle for a firefly when you could have the scorching sun? You deserve a better husband than this vagabond."

Enraged, Parvati retorted, "Brahmin! I thought you were wise, but I was mistaken. Everything you've said is a lie. Lord Shiva is a divine being with the power to appear in any form he chooses. He is, in fact, the embodiment of ParaBrahma, the supreme reality. ParaBrahma transcends emotions and responsibilities. He has no caste or clan because he is beyond all worldly distinctions. Lord Shiva is the one who assigned the divine duties to BrahmaDev and Vishnu, making him the supreme god of all. You mock his ashes, but did you know the Devas wear the ashes from Shiva's body on their foreheads as a mark of respect? I fear I've sinned just by listening to your words. If Lord Shiva does not marry me, I will remain a virgin for the rest of my life. I will not change my decision."

As the Brahmin was about to speak again, Parvati interrupted, "Stop! Don't say another word. I can't bear to hear your blasphemy. If you won't leave, I will move far away to avoid hearing any more of your insults."

The old Brahmin smiled and said, "My dear Devi, don't leave. I am captivated by your devotion."

Confused, Parvati looked closer at the Brahmin, who then transformed into the radiant form of Lord Shiva. Overwhelmed with shyness, she lowered her head.

Shining like the eternal sun, Lord Shiva said, "Devi, why did you leave me? Every minute without you felt like an eternity. Your devotion has filled me with bliss. But forgive me - I had to test your resolve. Now, I make you my wife. Come with me to Mount Kailas."

And so, with a grand ceremony attended by Himavat, Mena, and the Devas, Lord Shiva married Parvati, and they lived together as husband and wife on Mount Kailas.

9

KARTIKEYA

On Mount Kailas, Parvati became pregnant soon after her wedding to Lord Shiva. However, the fetus was so heavy that she struggled to bear its weight. Anilan, the God of Air, came to her aid. He removed the fetus from Parvati's body and delivered it to the Krittikas, who each carried a part of the fetus in six different wombs. The Krittikas is a group of six celestial nymphs.

As the fetus developed, the six Krittikas each gave birth to a baby. They placed the six infants together in a box and entrusted it to BrahmaDev. For years, BrahmaDev kept the box closed, until one day, the box opened from within, and a powerful child with six faces emerged. As he was nurtured by the Krittikas, he was named Kartikeya, and because of his six faces, he was also called Shanmugha.

When Parvati learned that her son had been born and was being raised by BrahmaDev and Saraswati, she said to Shiva, "Beloved, I long to see our son. Shall we visit him?"

Lord Shiva replied, "Devi Parvati, our son must remain with BrahmaDev for now, as he is destined to fulfill a prophecy. BrahmaDev will teach him the Vedas, sciences, and martial arts. We will visit him when the time is right."

Years later, when the appropriate time arrived, Shiva and Parvati visited BrahmaDev's abode. BrahmaDev welcomed them and called for Kartikeya. "Son, your parents are here. Salute them," he said.

Parvati rushed to embrace Kartikeya and, holding him tightly, said, "Come with us to Mount Kailas, my son."

But BrahmaDev intervened, "Devi, he is born to fulfill a prophecy. He will return to you once he has completed his destiny."

Kartikeya continued his training under BrahmaDev's guidance. Upon reaching adulthood, BrahmaDev presented him with a spear as a weapon and a peacock as his mode of transport. Once Kartikeya had mastered the arts of combat and sciences, he set out to challenge the demon Taraka.

Kartikeya marched to the gates of Taraka's fortress, leading an army of Devas. Meanwhile, Taraka had anticipated the attack and prepared his own army of Asuras.

Taunting the Devas, Taraka shouted, "You Devas never learn! You've lost before, and you will lose again. But the most laughable thing is that in your desperation, you've chosen a mere boy to lead you. Don't you know that only the son of Shiva can slay me?"

The battle began, and the ground trembled under the clash of warriors. While the Devas engaged the Asuras in combat, Kartikeya charged directly at Taraka. At first, Taraka dismissed Kartikeya as an ordinary teenage Deva, but as the fight progressed, he realized that Kartikeya was far stronger than he had anticipated.

The duel raged on for some time, and eventually, Kartikeya overpowered Taraka, knocking him to the ground. With his spear poised at Taraka's chest, the demon asked, "Who are you, boy?"

Kartikeya replied, "I am Kartikeya, son of Lord Shiva," and with that, he drove his spear through Taraka's heart, killing him.

Seeing the death of their leader, the Asuras fled the battlefield in fear, retreating to their dwellings. The Devas praised Kartikeya for fulfilling his destiny and restoring order to the universe. From that moment on, Kartikeya was revered as the God of War, and peace was restored across the three worlds, with none living in fear of another.

10

GANESH

When Parvati became pregnant with another child, Lord Shiva had to leave Mount Kailas with his Shivaganas to oversee the functioning of the universe. During his absence, Parvati gave birth to a radiant boy, whom she named *Ganesh*. Remarkably, Ganesh grew up faster than any other child in the universe, demonstrating immense intelligence and an unwavering commitment to any task he undertook.

One day, before heading to take a bath at Lake Manasarovar, Parvati called Ganesh and said, "My dear son, I am going to bathe in the lake, and I may enter deep meditation while there.

Ganesh

It is of utmost importance that I am not disturbed by anyone. It is your duty to stand guard and ensure no one passes through."

Ganesh bowed and replied, "Mother, I promise that no one shall pass as long as I live."

Satisfied with her son's reliability, Parvati left for the lake.

A short while later, Lord Shiva returned with his entourage and, as usual, wished to let Parvati know of his arrival. However, he was stopped by a strange boy standing guard.

"Stop! You are not allowed to pass!" Ganesh declared sternly.

Surprised, Lord Shiva asked, "What? A chubby child trying to stop me? Who are you?"

"It does not matter who I am. I have been ordered by Devi Parvati to guard this place and let no one through. I will carry out her orders without question," Ganesh replied firmly.

Shiva, slightly amused but also growing impatient, said, "You foolish boy! I am Shiva, the supreme God, Parvati's husband. I demand to see her."

"You may be Devi's husband or her father; it makes no difference to me. My duty is my highest honor, and I will not let you through," Ganesh said without compromise.

Shiva, now angered, shouted, "You have no idea who you are dealing with! Shivaganas, teach this child his place."

The Shivaganas attacked, but Ganesh defended his position with remarkable strength, holding his ground against them.

Shiva, watching the scene, thought, "Not even my mightiest followers can move this boy. He is stronger than I realized. It seems I must intervene myself."

With little effort, Lord Shiva pushed Ganesh aside, sending him flying. Shiva proceeded toward the lake without a second thought. However, determined and furious, Ganesh leapt back up and attempted to attack Shiva from behind. Reacting swiftly, Lord Shiva turned and, in a moment of rage, decapitated Ganesh with his weapon and reduced his head to ashes with his third eye.

Parvati, sensing something terrible had happened, rushed back, ending her bath. She found her son headless and covered in blood.

"My son! Who committed this outrageous act?" she cried.

A confused Lord Shiva asked, "Son? Is this... our son?"

Still weeping, Parvati replied, "Yes, he is our son. I had instructed him to guard me. I have lost him so soon after giving birth, and my heart cannot bear this."

Overcome with regret, Shiva said, "Beloved, I am the one responsible for this grave mistake. I thought he was just an arrogant boy teasing me. But do not fear, I will bring him back to life."

"But how?" Parvati asked. "He has lost his head."

"I have a solution," Shiva reassured her.

Shiva, along with his minions and Nandi, wandered through the forest in search of a way to restore Ganesh. Along the way, they came across a weeping elephant mourning the loss of her child.

Shiva, feeling empathy, said to the mother elephant, "I understand your grief. I will resurrect both of our departed children."

Shiva decapitated the dead elephant and placed its head on Ganesh's body. Using his divine power, he breathed life into the boy, and Ganesh was revived. Parvati showered blessings upon her son, and from that moment on, Ganesh became a symbol of auspiciousness, known for his faithfulness and wisdom.

Ganesh was not only devoted but also sharp-witted. One time, Lord Shiva and Parvati discussed the future of their children,

Kartikeya and Ganesh, as they had reached the age of marriage.

"Kartikeya and Ganesh are both equally beloved to us," Shiva said. "One is strong, and the other is wise. But I am unsure whose marriage we should arrange first."

Parvati responded, "Let us summon them and put them to the test."

Kartikeya and Ganesh approached their parents and listened attentively to their concerns.

"I am the elder, so I should be married first," Kartikeya declared.

"I am the wisest, so I should be married first," Ganesh countered.

Lord Shiva calmly responded, "You are both equal in our eyes. We do not judge you by age, strength, or intelligence. Therefore, we have decided to put you both to the test. The one who travels around the earth and returns here first will have the right to marry first."

As soon as Shiva finished, Kartikeya mounted his peacock and set off to circle the globe. Meanwhile, Ganesh sat down to think. "If I compete with Kartikeya in a race around the world, I will surely lose. I need a different approach."

After a brief moment of contemplation, Ganesh washed himself by a nearby lake, approached his parents, and said, "Dear mother and father, please take your seats on this platform I have prepared and bless me."

Shiva and Parvati, amused by his request, did as instructed. Ganesh then reverently worshiped them, walking around them seven times as one would circle a deity.

Smiling with satisfaction, Ganesh said, "Dear parents, I have completed the contest. I should be the first to marry."

Parvati, puzzled, replied, "My son, didn't we ask you to travel around the earth - across mountains, jungles, oceans, cities, and villages? But you have barely left this place."

Ganesh, slightly provoked, responded, "Beyond being my parents, you are the guardians of the world. Walking around you is equivalent to circling the earth itself. The divine Vedas teach that honoring one's parents in this manner is as meritorious as traveling the entire globe. If you declare me wrong, you declare the Vedas wrong. If I am not allowed to marry first, people will lose faith in the Vedas."

Amazed by his wisdom and logic, Lord Shiva said, "Dear son, you have outdone yourself. Every word you spoke is true. You have shown your deep understanding of the Vedas. Therefore, we will find a bride for you and arrange your marriage immediately."

As Shiva and Parvati began searching for a suitable bride, Prajapati Viswaroop approached them with news of his daughters, Siddhi and Buddhi. Siddhi, the personification of skill, and Buddhi, the personification of wisdom, were perfect matches for Ganesh. Delighted by the proposal, Shiva and Parvati arranged the marriage, which was held in the presence of Devas, rishis, and other dignitaries.

While Ganesh was happily living with his new wives, Kartikeya returned to Mount Kailas after his journey around the world. He learned about the events that had transpired from Sage Narada and was deeply disappointed. Feeling overshadowed, Kartikeya decided he could no longer remain with his parents. He left Mount Kailas and took up residence on Mount Krounch.

Wishing to see her son again, Parvati asked Shiva to visit Kartikeya. Together, they went to Mount Krounch, where they established their presence as divine idols. That place later became known as the sacred temple of Mallikarjuna, one of the twelve Jyotirlingas.

11

ANDHAKA

Lord Shiva and Devi Parvati were living a blissful married life, completely devoted to each other. They had no complaints and shared a deep bond of loyalty. However, one morning, Parvati woke up to find herself alone in bed. Lord Shiva returned later that afternoon. Parvati assumed he had left during the night to attend to some urgent matters and didn't dwell on it.

The next morning, the same thing happened. Parvati awoke to find Shiva missing again, only for him to return around noon. Her curiosity grew. Where was her husband going so early in the morning? Though she wanted to ask him directly, she hesitated, fearing it might seem like she didn't trust him.

Unable to shake her curiosity, Parvati decided to solve the mystery herself. She planned to stay awake and follow Shiva the next morning when he left. However, after staying up most of the night pretending to sleep, she accidentally dozed off just before dawn. When she woke up, Shiva was already gone. Blaming herself, she decided to search for him.

She looked everywhere near their abode but could find no sign of Shiva. Determined, Parvati ventured further into the distant mountains and valleys, asking everyone she met if they had seen her husband. No one had any useful answers. As noon approached and her search seemed futile, she spotted a group of Devas passing by.

"Respected Devas, have you seen my husband, Lord Shiva, anywhere?" Parvati asked.

"I saw him walking towards the next mountain early this morning," one of the Devas replied.

Thanking him, Parvati headed towards the indicated mountain. As she traveled through the valley, she noticed a dazzling light in the distance, so bright it made the sunlight seem dim in comparison. Intrigued, she approached the source and discovered it was coming from a cave. Parvati entered the cave to investigate and found that the radiant light was emanating from Lord Shiva, who was deep in Pranayama (meditative breathing).

For a moment, Parvati stood in awe, mesmerized by the sight. Then, overcome by passion and playfulness, she crept up behind Shiva and covered his eyes with her hands. Instantly, the radiant light vanished, plunging everything into darkness. A conch shell echoed through the cave as Shiva continued his Pranayama. Parvati's hands began to sweat, and as the drops of sweat fell to the ground, a sinister and ominous being was born from them. Since he was born in darkness, Shiva and Parvati named him "Andhaka."

Around the same time, an Asura named Hiranyaksha, who had long desired a son, had been worshipping Lord Shiva for a thousand years, praying for a child. Shiva appeared before him and said, "Noble Hiranyaksha, I am pleased with your devotion. What is your request?"

"My lord," Hiranyaksha replied, "I have longed for a child but have been unable to have one. I fear I may die without an heir. If you are truly pleased with me, I humbly ask that you grant me a son."

Moved by Hiranyaksha's plea, Shiva responded, "I understand the sorrow of being childless. Therefore, I will give you my own son, who was just born. His name is Andhaka. But I must warn you - if he ever becomes violent or causes harm to others, I will be the one to end his life."

Hiranyaksha, grateful for Shiva's gift, agreed to the terms and adopted Andhaka as his own, raising him in his kingdom.

Andhaka was raised as Hiranyaksha's own child, unaware that he had been adopted from Lord Shiva. As Andhaka grew, he developed the characteristics of a demon. His birth - born from the darkness and the sweat of Shiva and Parvati - and his upbringing among Asuras only added to his wicked nature.

Andhaka's actions terrorized the mortals of Earth. He delighted in committing horrific deeds such as destroying homes, burning ashrams, harming sages, setting fire to granaries, and harassing women. Despite Hiranyaksha's attempts to counsel him, Andhaka ignored all advice and continued his atrocities.

Turning his attention to Devaloka, Andhaka became obsessed with the beauty of the Apsaras and fantasized about keeping them for his personal pleasure. He even coveted Indrani, the wife of Lord Indra, desiring to make her his consort. While scheming, Andhaka and his minions came across a beautiful woman by the banks of the Ganga River. Captivated by her beauty, Andhaka declared that she was the most beautiful woman he had ever seen, not realizing that she was his own mother, Parvati.

"Who is that stunning woman?" Andhaka asked his minions.

"That is Parvati, the wife of Lord Shiva," one of them replied.

Another added, "How ironic it is that someone like Shiva, who is always surrounded by snakes and ghosts, should have such a beautiful wife. Surely, my lord Andhaka, she deserves a worthy husband like you."

Encouraged by their words, Andhaka exclaimed, "If that's the case, go and inform Parvati that the mighty Andhaka wishes to marry her."

Following his orders, the minions approached Parvati, who was playing with her companions, and conveyed Andhaka's proposal. Outraged, Parvati immediately informed Lord Shiva of the insult. Shiva, in his calm yet powerful manner, summoned the minions and said, "Tell your master that if he wishes to take Parvati as his wife, he must first defeat me in combat."

The minions returned to Andhaka with Shiva's message. Enraged, Andhaka grabbed his weapons and rushed to challenge Shiva. When the two met on the battlefield, Lord Shiva stood quietly, holding his trident, while Andhaka shouted vicious threats. Andhaka fired an arrow aimed at Shiva's head, but just as it was about to hit, Hiranyaksha intercepted it, sending it off course.

"Stop!" Hiranyaksha yelled. "Son, you have no idea of the sin you're about to commit!"

"Father, don't interfere with my destiny. You are shaming the Asura name!" Andhaka retorted.

"No, my son, you don't understand! Repent and fall at Lord Shiva's feet to ask for forgiveness," Hiranyaksha pleaded.

"Father, how can you ask me to bow before my enemy? You disgrace me."

With a heavy heart, Hiranyaksha finally revealed the truth. "Son, the one you are fighting is not your enemy; he is your true father - Lord Shiva. I am merely your foster father. You were given to me by Shiva after I prayed for a child. Parvati is your mother. Put down your weapons and beg for their forgiveness."

Hiranyaksha's words struck Andhaka like a bolt of lightning. He felt dizzy and weak, and the weapons slipped from his hands. Dropping to his knees, Andhaka thought, "Oh gods, what have I done?" His mind raced through all the sins he had committed, culminating in the ultimate one - desiring his own mother and attacking his father.

Andhaka walked slowly toward Lord Shiva, fell at his feet, and begged for forgiveness. "The only way I can be redeemed is by dying at your hands. Please forget that I am your son and treat me as a sinner. End my existence, for that is the only atonement I deserve."

Shiva lifted Andhaka and embraced him. "My son, you acted in ignorance, unaware that Parvati is your mother and I am your father. You are not a sinner, for you repented the moment you realized your mistake. By seeking forgiveness, you have already attained redemption. Go now, and apologize to your mother - she is waiting for you."

Andhaka approached Parvati and said, "Mother, if you do not forgive me, I have no choice but to end my life."

Parvati, full of compassion, replied, "Everyone in this world commits sin in one form or another. It is the sincerity of their apology that redeems them. I forgive you, my son."

Feeling relieved, Andhaka then turned to Shiva and requested, "I am still physically an Asura. Please bless me and free me from my demonic nature."

Shiva blessed him, saying, "From this moment, you will be an enlightened being. You are no longer an Asura. Instead, you shall become a guide for the Asuras, leading them on the path of righteousness."

Andhaka was transformed and became a devoted follower of Shiva, taking on the name Pungi, guiding others toward the path of virtue.

12

ASHOKASUNDARI

Once upon a time on Mount Kailas, Lord Shiva and Parvati were engaged in an intimate conversation. Shiva was describing the beauty of the universe and how it was created. He shared with her the story of the first days of creation. Curious, Parvati asked, "Beloved, I've been fortunate enough to witness many of the universe's most beautiful sights. I have always heard of the most magnificent garden in the world, but I have never seen it with my own eyes. Dear, which garden is that, and can you take me there?"

Shiva replied, "Devi, the most beautiful garden in the world is

Nandanavana. I will definitely take you there. It's a spectacular place that words cannot describe. You must experience it for yourself."

Fulfilling her wish, Lord Shiva took Parvati to Nandanavana. Parvati was enchanted by the breathtaking beauty of the garden, completely immersing herself in its splendour. She explored every corner of the garden, marvelling at each wondrous sight. As Parvati wandered through Nandanavana, she encountered its most magnificent feature. A tree radiating a brilliant aura.

"What is this mysterious tree?" Parvati asked.

"It is the legendary Kalpavriksha," Shiva explained. "It appeared during the churning of the ocean, the Samudra Manthan."

"Wow! It's extraordinary!" Parvati exclaimed in awe.

"There's more," Shiva added. "The Kalpavriksha can grant any wish."

Parvati approached the Kalpavriksha and said, "I have two sons, but, as a mother, I miss them dearly since they left our abode on Mount Kailas to fulfil their divine duties. I wish for a daughter who could ease my loneliness."

As soon as Parvati made her wish, a baby girl with a radiant glow appeared beneath the tree.

"Devi Parvati, look, your wish has been fulfilled," Shiva said.

Overjoyed, Parvati embraced the baby and exclaimed, "Let's name her!"

Shiva replied, "Yes, she will be called Ashokasundari."

Standing before the Kalpavriksha, Parvati looked at her daughter and said, "Ashokasundari, my dear daughter, you are destined to marry a man who is equal to Indra, the king of Devaloka."

Years passed, and Ashokasundari grew into a beautiful young woman. One day, as she wandered through Nandanavana with her maids, a Rakshasa named Hunda spotted her. He thought to himself, "What stunning beauty! She must be mine!"

Hunda approached Ashokasundari and said, "Hey, beautiful! You should consider yourself fortunate to be desired by a powerful being like me. I would be honoured to take you as my wife."

Ashokasundari retorted, "You pitiful Rakshasa! I don't need you. My destiny is to marry a man who is equal to Indra, the ruler of the heavens. His name is Nahusha, and there is no way I will marry you."

Angered by her rejection, Hunda left but soon devised a plan. Disguising himself as a widow whose husband he had killed, he approached Ashokasundari again. "Oh, kind girl, I am alone and too frightened to return to my home. Will you please accompany me to my hermitage?"

Unaware of the deception, Ashokasundari replied, "Of course, I'll gladly help you."

The goddess accompanied the disguised Hunda to what she thought was a hermitage but was actually Hunda's palace. Realizing too late that she had been tricked, Ashokasundari shouted, "You vile demon! You think you can trap me here? I curse you. You will die at the hands of Nahusha!"

Ashokasundari then escaped and returned to her parents' abode on Mount Kailas.

Meanwhile, Nahusha was growing up under the care of Maharshi Vasishta. As he matured, Nahusha became a powerful warrior and learned about his destiny to defeat Hunda, the Rakshasa. He soon discovered that Hunda had abducted Ashokasundari again. Determined to fulfil his destiny and rescue her, Nahusha rushed to Hunda's palace.

After a fierce battle, Nahusha defeated Hunda and freed Ashokasundari. As foretold, the two were married. In time, Nahusha rose to become the supreme regent of Devaloka, fulfilling his great destiny.

13

SHASTHA

After the death of her brother Mahishasura, Karambhika vowed to take revenge on the Devas. To achieve this, she travelled to the Vindhya mountain range and began a rigorous penance. Her meditation lasted for years until BrahmaDev appeared before her.

He said, "Karambhika, I am deeply pleased with your devotion. You may ask for a boon."

She replied, "Grant me invincibility. Let no one have the power to kill me."

BrahmaDev responded, "That is impossible. Everyone must meet their end one day. That is the universal law. However, I can make you nearly invincible, but only if you specify who can kill you."

Karambhika thought for a moment and said, "Alright then, Deva. Only the son of Shiva and Vishnu should be able to kill me. Moreover, he must be born and live as a human on earth to attain that power."

BrahmaDev granted her wish. Karambhika, feeling triumphant, thought, "I am virtually invincible now. How can Shiva and Vishnu have a child together? It's absurd!" Confident in her safety, she began her campaign of terror against the Devas.

Meanwhile, Lord Shiva had heard about Vishnu's transformation into Mohini, a beautiful damsel used to deceive the Asuras during the churning of the ocean, Samudra Manthan. Though Shiva had never seen Mohini, he had heard much about her beauty and charm, which could captivate any man.

Curious, Shiva went to Vishnu and said, "Vishnu, I've heard a lot about your disguise as Mohini. Is it true that you can enchant anyone with it?"

Vishnu replied, "Yes, it's true. As Mohini, I can lure anyone. They forget everything around them and become completely enchanted by my presence. The Maya of Mohini is so powerful that no one can resist it."

Shiva was sceptical. "Even I wouldn't be able to resist?" he asked.

"I doubt it," Vishnu responded.

Shiva insisted, "Then show me. Prove it."

Vishnu hesitated but eventually agreed. "Are you sure?" he asked.

"Yes," Shiva confirmed. "It's worth testing."

Without further delay, Vishnu transformed into Mohini. Soon,

Shiva found himself utterly captivated by her irresistible beauty and charm. The Maya was so overwhelming that even Shiva could not resist its pull. Entranced by Mohini's allure, Shiva embraced her, and Mohini responded in kind. From their brief union, a child was born.

Shiva declared, "Since this child is born from the union of the two mightiest gods, he will be the most powerful among all beings. He shall be known as Shastha. He will descend to earth to fulfil his destiny."

As foretold, baby Shastha appeared in a jungle on earth. Coincidentally, it was the same place where the king of Pandalam was hunting. Upon hearing the cry of the baby, the king sent his troops to investigate. There, lying on the ground, they found the divine child.

The king said, "This is no ordinary child. He has divine qualities. Surely, he is a gift from the gods. He shall be raised in the royal palace, and I will name him Manikanta."

Manikanta was brought up in the palace of the Pandalam kingdom, enjoying all the royal privileges. He was trained in the military arts and became an expert in various fields, including arts, sciences, and martial arts. The king eventually decided that Manikanta was the ideal successor to the throne.

Years passed, and when Manikanta turned twelve, the king made plans to formally declare him the heir. However, the queen, influenced by an evil minister, had different plans.

The minister whispered to the queen, "Why should you allow the king to make some orphaned tribal boy the prince when you have your own son? You must object to the king's decision."

The queen, swayed by his words, said, "You are right! This injustice cannot continue. My son deserves the throne."

The minister thought to himself, "Ha ha, my plan is falling into place. The queen's biological son is incapable of ruling. With no powerful leader, I will seize control of the kingdom myself."

The queen approached the king and asked, "Why do you plan to crown Manikanta as your heir?"

The king replied, "Because he is deserving. He would sacrifice anything for the welfare of others."

The queen, feigning concern, said, "Is that so? The royal physicians claim that only tiger's milk can cure my illness, but no one is brave enough to fetch it. Why don't you ask Manikanta? If he succeeds, he will prove his worth and truly deserve to be your heir."

The king confidently replied, "I will ask him. I am certain he will agree."

As the king left, the queen smirked and thought to herself, "Foolish boy. He will surely be killed by the wild animals."

When Manikanta heard of the task, he volunteered to retrieve the tiger's milk and set off into the forest. There, he encountered several Devas.

They greeted him, saying, "Oh, you are the great Shastha. We are overjoyed to see you."

Manikanta, confused, replied, "Who are you, divine beings? My name is Manikanta."

The Devas then revealed his true identity, explaining the prophecy and his divine origins.

They added, "An Asura named Karambhika is terrorizing us. Only you can defeat her."

Determined, Manikanta advanced to face Karambhika. A fierce battle began.

Karambhika taunted, "You fool! Your efforts are in vain. Only the son of Shiva and Vishnu can destroy me."

Manikanta calmly responded, "For your information, I am that son - Shastha, Manikanta, or HariHaraSuthan. Call me by any name you wish, but your end has come."

Without delay, Manikanta annihilated Karambhika. The Devas rejoiced and said, "Dear Shastha, you have fulfilled the prophecy. Come with us to Devalok."

Manikanta, however, declined. "No, I still have unfinished duties on Earth."

Meanwhile, back in Pandalam, the king grew anxious. Days had passed without any word from Manikanta. The queen and her minister were secretly pleased, expecting the worst. To their astonishment, Manikanta returned to the court, carrying the tiger's milk.

He announced, "Here is the tiger's milk you asked for. I hope it cures your illness."

The king, overjoyed, said, "Dear Manikanta, you don't need to go anywhere else. You should be the king of Pandalam."

Manikanta respectfully declined. "Father, I am sorry, but I cannot accept your offer. I have chosen a spiritual path over a royal one. But fear not, I will protect not just this kingdom, but all humanity from harm."

Thus, Shastha lived the rest of his life as a hermit in the mountains of Sabarimala, where he became widely known as Ayyappan.

14

JALANDHARA

Once upon a time, Indra and Brihaspati journeyed to Mount Kailas to meet Lord Shiva. Knowing of their visit beforehand, Shiva disguised himself as a Yogi with matted hair and a radiant face, intending to test their knowledge and devotion. The Yogi stood in their path, stretching his arms out to block their way.

Indra, not recognizing the Yogi's true identity, became furious and shouted, "Who are you? Where do you come from? Make way for us!"

The Yogi remained silent, unmoved by Indra's commands.

Growing more impatient, Indra repeated his demands, ordering the Yogi to step aside. When the Yogi still refused to budge, Indra's anger boiled over, and he aimed his thunderbolt at the Yogi. However, the Yogi effortlessly subdued the thunderbolt, standing firm with eyes blazing red in fury. Shiva's third eye began to open, signalling an impending firebolt.

Suddenly, Brihaspati recognized the Yogi as Lord Shiva. Falling at his feet, he pleaded, "Dear Lord, please forgive Indra for his rudeness. He acted out of ignorance, not knowing it was you. I beg you, my Lord, spare his life and pardon his behaviour."

Lord Shiva, still enraged, replied, "I can control my anger and refrain from killing Indra, but the energy for his destruction has already been gathered. It must be discharged from my body."

Brihaspati pleaded further, "Lord of all, please save Indra by releasing the firebolt elsewhere."

Shiva, now calm, said, "I am pleased with your devotion, Brihaspati. I will heed your request. I shall cast this fire of destruction far away from Indra."

Shiva discharged the fire from his third eye into the ocean. When the firebolt struck the water, the ocean and fire combined to create a child. The baby's cry was so powerful that it shook the entire world. Brahma descended from his abode to investigate the source of the sound. The ocean god, Sagara, approached Brahma and said, "O BrahmaDev! I do not know where this boy came from, but as he was born on my lap, it is my duty to raise him. Can you name him and declare his future?"

Brahma took the child into his lap, but as soon as he did, the boy strangled him, choking him. In pain, a tear fell from Brahma's eye. Managing to put the boy down, Brahma declared, "This child will be known as Jalandhara, for he has brought water from my eyes. He will master both science and martial arts and grow to be an unbeatable conqueror. Not even Vishnu will be able to defeat him. However, there is one condition: Jalandhara will remain invincible only as long as his wife remains chaste."

A relieved Sagara took the boy back to his palace and raised him as his own. Jalandhara grew into a handsome and exceptionally powerful man, regarded as one of the mightiest Asuras. With his foster father's blessings, he married Vrinda, the daughter of the Asura Kalameni. Inspired by Jalandhara's strength, many Asuras who had been hiding in Patala after their defeat by the Devas resurfaced.

Jalandhara was crowned emperor of the Asuras, ruling justly and with dignity under the guidance of his teacher, Shukracharya. Over time, Jalandhara learned the stories of how Hiranyakashipu and Hiranyaksha had been defeated, how Vishnu had severed Rahu's head, and how the Asuras had been cheated by the Devas during the Samudra Manthan. Resenting these injustices, Jalandhara vowed to take revenge on the Devas and Vishnu for oppressing the Asuras.

He declared an all-out war on the Devas and led an invasion of Devalok. A ferocious battle ensued, with heavy casualties on both sides. However, the Asuras, under Jalandhara's leadership, held the advantage. The Devas, unprepared for such a formidable foe, struggled. Shukracharya resurrected fallen Asuras using his Mritsanjivani potion, while Brihaspati revived the dead Devas using medicinal herbs from Mount Drongiri.

Shukracharya advised Jalandhara to destroy the mountain to prevent Brihaspati from accessing the herbs. Jalandhara, following the advice, attacked Brihaspati and plunged the mountain into chaos.

Certain of their defeat, the Devas sought Lord Vishnu's help. Upon hearing their plea, Lakshmi, who was also the daughter of the ocean god Sagara, begged Vishnu, "Dear VishnuDev, my husband, I request you not to harm my brother Jalandhara."

Vishnu replied, "I cannot remain idle while the world descends into chaos because of your brother. I must intervene, but I promise you I won't kill Jalandhara."

A fierce battle raged between Jalandhara and Lord Vishnu for a long time. Eventually, Vishnu realized that he could not defeat Jalandhara. To avoid prolonging the fight, Vishnu said, "Jalandhara, I propose a truce. If you agree to stop fighting me, I will grant you any wish you desire."

A cunning Jalandhara replied, "O valiant Vishnu, make Ksheera Sagara your home. Be my guest and live at my abode forever."

Vishnu agreed and began residing there with Lakshmi. However, it was more like house arrest for Vishnu, as the entire Ksheera Sagara was under Jalandhara's control.

With Vishnu trapped and unable to help, the Devas were ultimately defeated by the Asuras. Jalandhara was declared emperor of the three worlds, and the Devas were devastated by the humiliation of being ruled by the Asuras. Desperate, Narada and the Devas devised a plan to overthrow Jalandhara. After consulting with them, Narada went to meet Jalandhara at his palace.

Narada said, "O mighty king Jalandhara, I am truly astonished by your achievements. You have conquered the entire world, including Devalok. But I am disappointed that you have not yet conquered Kailas. Perhaps you haven't heard about it. Kailas, where Lord Shiva resides, is unparalleled in beauty. There is no other place that can match it."

Jalandhara responded, "Kailas may not have the treasures I possess here."

Narada slyly added, "Perhaps, but rumours suggest that you lack the power to conquer Kailas."

Infuriated, Jalandhara gathered his massive army and marched to Kailas, surrounding the sacred mountain. Nandi led Lord Shiva's forces against the invaders, but the army suffered heavy losses. Accompanied by Virabhadra, Lord Shiva entered the battlefield. Kartikeya joined the fight but was overwhelmed, and even Ganesha was defeated by Jalandhara. Overpowered by the Asura army, Shiva wondered why he was unable to triumph.

At that moment, BrahmaDev informed Parvati of Jalandhara's boon that he would remain invincible as long as his wife, Vrinda, remained chaste. During the intense battle, Parvati approached Vishnu and relayed what Brahma had told her, pleading for his help.

With his divine powers of illusion, Vishnu disguised himself as Jalandhara. He created the illusion that Jalandhara had been killed by Shiva and then resurrected. In this guise, Vishnu visited Vrinda, who embraced him, believing him to be her husband. As a result, Vrinda unknowingly lost her chastity.

When Vrinda realized she had been tricked and that it was Vishnu in disguise, she cursed him, saying, "One day, someone will abduct your wife as you have deceived me." Heartbroken, Vrinda then immolated herself in a fire.

Meanwhile, Jalandhara's army began to falter, suffering heavy losses. Ultimately, his warriors either lay dead or fled the battlefield. Jalandhara then personally engaged Lord Shiva in combat. Shiva pierced Jalandhara's chest with his Trishul, but the Asura did not die immediately. Sensing this, Shiva struck the ocean with his toe, creating a divine chakra (discus). Using this chakra, he beheaded Jalandhara, finally killing him.

Many years later, Lord Shiva gifted this chakra to Vishnu, and it became known as the Sudarshana Chakra.

15

RAKTAJA

Once in Devalok, Vishnu and Brahma were discussing celestial beings and their powers. Their conversation soon shifted to the philosophies and moral duties of maintaining balance in the universe. At one point, Vishnu boasted, "Without me, the whole world would have fallen apart by now. I perform the divine act of preservation."

Brahma did not appreciate this claim. He responded, "Preservation isn't such a great feat. I am responsible for creating life. Without me, there would be nothing for you to preserve in the first place."

Their conversation took a contentious turn as both began asserting their superiority. Brahma declared, "I create everything in this world. Undoubtedly, I am far superior to you."

Vishnu thought, "I can't believe Brahma's arrogance. He was born from the lotus that sprouted from my navel. Even his very dwelling originated from my body, yet he dares to boast that he is the ultimate God."

Vishnu then asked, "Brahma, how can you claim to be greater than me when you originated from my body?"

Brahma had no real answer, but he was unwilling to admit defeat. Standing firm, he refused to back down. Vishnu continued to question him about his origins, but Brahma, in his pride, decided to lie. He boldly declared, "I did not originate from your body, nor did Shiva create me. I was the first to take form in this universe, and I created all of you."

Stunned by Brahma's blatant lie, Vishnu called upon Lord Shiva to settle the dispute. Shiva arrived promptly and asked Brahma, "Brahma, I hear you've been spreading lies. Tell me, how did you come into being?"

Brahma replied, "It is as clear as daylight. I was the first to appear in this world, and I created the rest of the universe, including you."

Hearing this, Shiva burst into a furious rage. Losing his composure, he shouted, "How dare you lie to me, Brahma?"

Overcome with anger, Shiva plucked one of Brahma's five heads from his body and disappeared, taking the severed head with him. Brahma, writhing in agony, was left in great pain. Though he still had four heads, the loss of one was excruciating. In his anguish and fury, Brahma began to sweat profusely. He wiped the sweat from his forehead and threw it to the ground.

Brahma shouted, "Let a mighty Asura be born to punish Shiva for decapitating me!"

Instantly, from the fallen sweat, a giant Asura clad in a thousand armours was born. His name was Swedaja, but because of his thousand armours, he became known as Sahasrakavacha.

Brahma commanded, "Swedaja, avenge me. Kill Shiva, who has humiliated me!"

Obeying his creator, Swedaja charged toward Mount Kailas. Shiva, aware that he couldn't face the might of this powerful Asura alone, sought Vishnu's help.

"I must now face this monster because I defended you during your argument with Brahma," Shiva said to Vishnu. "Therefore, you are obligated to help me."

Vishnu agreed. As Swedaja approached, Vishnu leaped to defend Shiva. A fierce battle erupted, but Swedaja's strength proved overwhelming. Vishnu, realizing he needed a greater force, let out a mighty roar, and its vibrations were so powerful that they knocked Swedaja to the ground, rendering him unconscious.

"It seems the Asura will regain consciousness any moment now," Vishnu said, "and when he does, he will surely kill me as well."

Shiva replied, "We need to come up with something else."

Vishnu extended his right arm toward Shiva. "All I can do is offer you my arm," he said. "Do with it as you see fit."

After a brief moment of thought, Shiva pierced Vishnu's arm with his Trishul. Blood began to flow profusely, pooling on the ground. Shiva focused his third eye on the blood, and a firebolt struck it, causing the blood to bubble. From the bubbling blood, a giant crowned being with a thousand arms arose. As he was born from blood, he was named Raktaja.

Shiva announced, "Vishnu, this mighty being was born from your blood and the fire of my third eye. He is invincible and will defend us with bravery."

Raktaja bowed to Shiva and said, "Master! Command me as you wish."

Shiva replied, "Raktaja, awaken the unconscious Swedaja and annihilate him."

Without hesitation, Raktaja charged toward Swedaja. The thunderous sound of Raktaja's roar startled Swedaja awake. Annoyed at the sight of the thousand-armed giant standing before him, Swedaja leaped to attack, and a fierce battle ensued. The fight raged on for many years without a decisive outcome. Neither combatant was willing to retreat. Swedaja lost all but one of his thousand armours, while Raktaja lost all but one of his arms. Despite their losses, both continued the fight.

Brahma, Vishnu, and Shiva watched the epic battle like bewildered spectators. Finally, Vishnu turned to Brahma and said, "Brahma, command them to stop. This battle could go on for years, and it is disturbing the peace of the heavens. Raktaja is certain to kill Swedaja."

Brahma replied, "That is unlikely. Raktaja cannot defeat Swedaja in this life. Perhaps in the next life, he can."

Vishnu nodded. "Then let them resolve this in their next life. Their fight here in Devalok is disrupting the cosmic order."

Thus, the Trimurti addressed the battling giants: "Swedaja and Raktaja, cease your fight immediately. You may continue your battle in your next lives as humans, and there, a victor will be declared."

The giants agreed to the truce. As foretold, Swedaja was reborn as Karna and Raktaja as Arjuna during the Dwapara Yuga. Their rivalry resumed during their human lives. Vishnu incarnated as Krishna to aid Arjuna, and in the Mahabharata War, Karna was ultimately defeated by Arjuna.

16

GANGADHARA

One day, King Sagara conducted a Yaga for the welfare of his kingdom. An essential part of the Yaga was a horse. Unfortunately, the horse was stolen by Indra, who was jealous of Sagara's power. In response, Sagara assigned all sixty thousand of his sons to search the world for the missing horse. Indra had tied the horse near the ashram of sage Kapil in Patala to divert the blame.

Eventually, Sagara's sons found the horse near Rishi Kapil, who was meditating. Assuming that the sage had stolen the horse, they began to insult him and disturb his meditation. Maharshi

Kapil opened his eyes and discovered that the sons of Sagara were disrupting his penance. Enraged, Kapil burned all sixty thousand sons of Sagara to death with a single glance.

Unfortunately, the souls of Sagara's sons suffered an unfortunate fate, as their final spiritual rites were not performed. This left their souls wandering, unable to attain Moksha. To ensure their liberation, Anshuman, their nephew, began praying to Brahma to deliver Ganga, the divine and cosmic river, to Earth. However, his prayers were in vain.

At that moment, Anshuman's son Dilip also tried to bring Ganga to Earth but failed as well. Years passed, and Dilip's son, Bhagiratha, learned about the history of his ancestors. "It is my destiny to bring Ganga to Earth so that her waters can cleanse the souls of my ancestors and liberate them to heaven," Bhagiratha thought. "The purpose of my existence lies in this duty."

Bhagiratha began a meditation that lasted for years. Finally, pleased with Bhagiratha's prayers, Brahma appeared before him and said, "Bhagiratha, what is it that you truly need? Do you desire wealth, power, or a consort?"

To this, Bhagiratha replied, "I do not wish for anything for my personal pleasure. However, I request you to bring the divine celestial river Ganga to Earth so that she can cleanse the souls of my ancestors and help the generations that follow."

Brahma said, "All I can do is convey your message to Ganga. I will inform her of the need for her presence here on Earth. I am sure she will agree."

Brahma approached Ganga, who was flowing through the cosmic sphere. He said, "Dear Ganga, it is of utmost importance that you abandon your presence here and begin flowing through the terrains of Earth. The Moksha of thousands of beings depends on it."

Offended, Ganga replied, "My existence is not to be dictated by the wishes of mortals. Brahma, your orders violate my sense of freedom. However, out of respect for you, I will descend to Earth. But let Bhagiratha know that my arrival will be so forceful that the impact may shatter the Earth and its inhabitants."

Brahma then appeared before Bhagiratha and said, "Dear Bhagiratha, I have both good news and bad news. The good news is that Ganga has agreed to come to Earth. The bad news is that her descend will be so devastating that the Earth may not withstand it. Therefore, you must find a solution to ensure the safety of the Earth; otherwise, everyone will blame you for the destruction."

Anxious and troubled, Bhagiratha began praying to Lord Shiva, knowing that only he could help at this critical moment.

Lord Shiva appeared and said, "O kind devotee, I am pleased with your worship. Let me know your wish, and I can grant it."

Bhagiratha requested, "O almighty God of all, for the sake of my ancestors and future generations, I have implored Ganga to descend to Earth for her divine presence. But the impact of her plunge may destroy the Earth. I request you to save it from such a fate."

Shiva replied, "I will gladly take up this task, for you have made a selfless request."

Lord Shiva waited for Ganga's descend. He saw her approaching and prepared for the point of impact. Ganga fell arrogantly onto Shiva's head. However, Shiva calmly trapped her in his locks of hair and released her in small streams. This act further enhanced Ganga's divinity. As Ganga flowed to Patala, she carved out a diverse stream to remain on Earth, helping to cleanse the unfortunate souls residing there. Ganga became the only river to flow through all three worlds - Devalok, Earth, and Patala. Thus, she also came to be known as Tripathaga, the one who travels the three worlds.

Bhagiratha became renowned for his unconditional efforts,

and his name became synonymous with hard work. The phrase "Bhagirath prayatna" is used to describe valiant efforts or difficult achievements. Meanwhile, Lord Shiva earned the name "Gangadhara" for holding Ganga upon her arrival on Earth.

17

KALI AND RAKTABIJA

Raktabija, the king of the Asuras, sought to wage war upon the Devas and conquer the three worlds. His ambitions mirrored the ultimate dream of every Asura warlord before him. Nonetheless, he knew he needed to become more powerful than ever to achieve his desires. Thus, Raktabija devoted himself to meticulous penance toward BrahmaDev.

Finally, BrahmaDev appeared before Raktabija and said, "Hey, Raktabija! Your prayers have pleased me. Ask for any wish, and I will grant it."

The Asura replied, "Dear BrahmaDev, make me immortal and invincible!"

Brahma responded, "It is impossible, Raktabija. Every being in the universe has a beginning and an end. Immortality is non-existent. You can ask for anything else besides this impractical request and I can surely grant you that."

Raktabija said, "Since I cannot attain immortality, let me request not to be slain by a man, the Devas, or the great Trimurti. If death must conquer me, it can only approach me through a woman. Women are feeble and powerless. If you grant me this boon, I will be virtually immortal."

Brahma replied, "Hey, king of Asuras. Your wish is granted. You shall become the most powerful being among men and gods. However, I cannot guarantee that you will be immortal. There is no escaping fate." After granting the boon, Brahma disappeared.

Raktabija returned to his kingdom, confident in his newfound invincibility. He dispatched an army of Asuras to invade neighbouring kingdoms. His tyrannical army subdued all opposition, and soon Raktabija became the tyrant of the entire earth.

After his conquest of earth was complete, Raktabija announced to his generals and the Asura army, "The Asura clan has proved its bravery in warfare and gained sufficient experience to advance towards our ultimate objective. For ages, the Devas have occupied Devlok, spending their days in luxury while we have been banished to the dark underworld of Patala. We must take vengeance for this injustice. I am invincible and virtually immortal. The gods can never kill me. Let the arrangements be made. We shall invade Devlok immediately and defeat Indra."

At daybreak the next day, Raktabija ordered his army to march to Devlok. When Indra heard about the impending attack, he assembled a council of key Devas, including Vayu, Varuna, Agni, and Yama.

Indra said, "Raktabija, the Asura chief, is marching to conquer us at this very moment. We have two options: either to meet him in combat or to accept him as our autocrat and become his vassals."

The Devas decided to accept war and fight back. The egotistical Devas could never even consider surrendering to their nemesis without a battle. Yet, they needed some blessings to defend against the mighty Asura army. Therefore, the Devas visited Lord Brahma and prayed for his help against Raktabija and his forces. BrahmaDev said, "I have granted Raktabija the boon that he cannot be killed by anyone except a woman. I do not have the power to harm him. Let us go to Mt. Kailas and ask Lord Shiva for his assistance in this battle."

Subsequently, the Devas, along with Brahma, went to Shiva's dwelling and prayed for his protection of IndraDev and the rest of the Devas against the ravaging Asuras. Lord Shiva instructed them to approach Vishnu for help. Thus, the Devas went to Lord Vishnu, who confirmed his assistance.

The armies of Devas and Asuras fiercely met on the battlefield. As soon as Raktabija saw one of his soldiers fall in combat, he became enraged and renewed his vigour. Indra fired an arrow at Raktabija, striking him in the heart. The Devas shouted with joy at witnessing the fall of the Asura leader, while the demoralized Asura warriors cried out and began to flee.

However, to the astonishment of all the Devas, the fallen Raktabija stood back up without succumbing to death. Moreover, from the blood gushing from his wounded body, a thousand clones of Raktabija emerged.

Raktabija shouted, "Stupid Devas! You can't kill me. A thousand clones of my image will rise from each drop of my blood. So think twice before attacking me!"

Hearing this, the overjoyed Asuras charged into the battlefield, shouting praises of Raktabija. Confused, the Devas shot another arrow at Raktabija, and as expected, a thousand more Raktabijas spawned from the blood splattered by the resulting wound.

Without delay, Vishnu entered the arena, prepared for war. When he saw that the Devas were being overwhelmed, he faced Raktabija himself. He struck Raktabija on the head with his mace, and the force of the blow sent Raktabija crashing to the ground. Yet he swiftly regained consciousness. Frustrated, Vishnu attempted to behead him with the Sudarsanachakra. However, as soon as Raktabija was decapitated, a new head grew back on his body, and millions of clones emerged from the flood of blood. Realizing that his efforts against Raktabija were ineffective, Vishnu retreated from the battle.

When the Devas saw that Vishnu had vanished from the battlefield, they realized their efforts would be futile. Disheartened, IndraDev tried to motivate them, but they were already in agony and panic. They could no longer battle as efficiently as before. Unable to withstand the relentless assault, the Devas fled from the battle in confusion. The valiant Devas deserted their posts and ran away, including Indra himself.

Raktabija's unassailable army stormed Devlok, and Raktabija declared himself the king of the heavens. He appointed his most trusted Asuras to the positions formerly held by the foremost Devas. Meanwhile, the Devas, having fled from the heavens, approached BrahmaDev and begged for advice on how to reclaim their lost sovereignty.

Brahma said, "My dear Devas, I am helpless. Raktabija is unbeatable by any man, Deva, or even the almighty Trimurti. However, a woman can kill him. Let's go to Mt. Kailas and seek Lord Shiva's help. He might have a solution to our problem."

The council of Devas, along with BrahmaDev and Lord Vishnu, visited Mt. Kailas, where they found Lord Shiva and Parvati waiting for them.

Vishnu said, "Dear Lord, you must be aware of the recent

events. The Asuras, under Raktabija, have conquered the three worlds, and the Devas have been driven from their kingdom. Strengthened by his boon, Raktabija believes he is invincible, and he has unleashed a reign of terror. He can only be killed by a woman. Do you know of any woman capable of defeating this evil Asura?"

Upon hearing this, Lord Shiva turned to Parvati and said, "Devi, the time has come for you to unleash your power."

A shocked Parvati replied, "Oh no! I cannot. I mustn't."

"The fate of the universe depends on your decision, Devi. It must be done," Shiva urged.

"But, my Lord, it is uncontrollable. I may become a threat to the world itself," Parvati protested.

"There is no other way. Do not worry about losing control. I will ensure the world is not harmed," Shiva reassured her.

As Parvati slipped from Shiva's grasp and descended into the abyss, Shiva shouted to the Devas, "Brace yourselves! Let's hope the price won't be too high."

Parvati, the reincarnation of Sati, is none other than the almighty Goddess ParaSakti. The various forms of Shakti lay dormant within her, awaiting the moment when they would be summoned. When necessary, Parvati could transform into these powerful beings, but at a cost. Once this transformation occurred, Parvati would fall into a deep trance, overpowered by the prevailing force. Awakening Parvati from this state was nearly impossible. And thus, with a deafening roar, the mighty warrior goddess Kali rose.

In awe, the Devas cried, "Salutations, almighty mother, salutations to you. Save us from the havoc of the evil Asura, Raktabija. He cannot be slain by anyone but you. Kill him and restore us to our rightful place in Devlok. You are our only hope!"

Kali charged towarda Raktabija's fort with a roar so powerful it caused the ground to tremble. Asuras were dispatched to investigate the source of the tumultuous noise and were ordered to detain the invader. But when the soldiers saw the fearsome Goddess advancing, they were struck with terror and fled back to Raktabija.

Raktabija ordered a large band of soldiers to attack the intruder, but all were annihilated by Kali singlehandedly. In disbelief, Raktabija looked out at the battlefield before his fort and saw a pitch-black woman adorned with a garland of skulls approaching. Realizing that this formidable being was a woman, Raktabija panicked but gathered his courage and prepared to face Kali himself.

Raktabija hurled giant boulders at Kali, but she shattered them to dust. He ran to her and attempted to stab her, but Kali struck him with her trident, and he collapsed, bleeding profusely. Despite the wound, Raktabija laughed and let out a deafening roar.

"You fool!" Raktabija shouted. "Thousands of Raktabijas will spawn from the blood you shed. This will be your end!"

But to his shock, Kali began drinking the blood before it could reach the ground. She stabbed him again with her trident, and though blood splattered, she drank every drop. Raktabija stood frozen in fear.

As the final blow, Kali beheaded Raktabija with her disc and drank all the blood that gushed from his body, bringing an end to the Asura. The dismayed Asura army fled back to Patala, abandoning Devlok. The Devas rejoiced and prepared to reoccupy their places in Devlok. However, Lord Shiva cautioned, "It's not over yet. Kali must be controlled, or her rage will destroy the entire universe."

Kali began her victory dance among the Asura corpses. Her steps made the ground crumble, and her roars filled the sky. Her terrifying laughter echoed throughout the heavens, drawing the attention of the Devas. They watched in astonishment as Kali's dance grew more intense, her feet causing destruction with every step. It became clear that this could lead to the apocalypse unless something was done. The Devas begged Lord Shiva to intervene and stop Kali before it was too late.

Lord Shiva said, "Kali cannot be stopped. She will only calm down once her victory dance is complete."

The Devas, alarmed, responded, "But Lord, the world cannot endure much more. It will be crushed under a few more of Kali's steps."

Shiva called out to Parvati, but she could not hear him, as Kali had completely taken over. The Parvati within her lay deep in slumber. Kali whipped her hair wildly, causing storms to sweep away some of the Devas. She lifted her arms to the sky, laughing maniacally. Nothing could stop this display of raw power.

Shiva called out again, but his words were drowned out. In a final, desperate act to save the world, Lord Shiva threw himself beneath Kali's dancing feet. She continued her turbulent dance, but this time, Shiva acted as her platform. The Devas watched anxiously, fearing that this could be the end of Lord Shiva. Yet, the steps that had previously shaken the world were now absorbed by Shiva's body. Only the almighty Lord Shiva could endure such pain.

After a few moments, Kali realized that it was her husband, Shiva, lying beneath her feet. The Parvati within Kali slowly awoke, taking control of her body. As Kali slipped into slumber, Parvati fully regained consciousness.

With tears in her eyes, Parvati said, "Oh dear husband, did I hurt you? What have I done?"

Lord Shiva replied, "No, Devi. You have saved the world. We are all thankful to you."

The Devas sighed in relief and expressed their gratitude to Parvati and Shiva for their intervention.

Thus, through Lord Shiva's swift and gallant actions, Kali's dance of destruction was neutralized, and Parvati returned. With the world now safe, the Devas reclaimed their places in Devlok.

18

THE FALL OF TRIPURA

The three sons of Tarakasura, Tarakaksha, Vidyunmali, and Kamalaksha, were consumed with intense grief following their father's death at the hands of Kartikeya. Tarakaksha, the eldest, was followed by his younger brothers, Vidyunmali and Kamalaksha. Although they were devoted worshippers of Lord Shiva, they harboured deep hatred toward the Devas, believing them to be responsible for orchestrating their father's demise.

Determined to avenge their father's death, the three brothers left behind their royal comforts and retreated to a cave on

Mount Meru, where they began a severe penance to please Brahma. Their penance continued for a thousand years, until Brahma finally appeared before them.

Brahma said, "Dear Asuras, I am pleased with your devotion. Those who worship me shall not be disappointed. Tell me, why have you undertaken such a long and arduous penance? What boon do you seek? Ask for what you desire, and I will grant it."

The Asuras replied, "Great BrahmaDev, you are very generous. We are honoured that you have accepted us as your devotees. Please grant us the boon of immortality. We wish never to be killed by anyone, to be protected from disease and old age, and to be invincible and unassailable."

Brahma was astonished by their request. After considering it for a moment, he said, "Mighty Asuras, immortality is impossible. Even the supreme gods must die one day. Everyone must meet their end in some way, as it is an inevitable part of the universe. Therefore, I cannot grant you this wish. However, you may ask for any other boon."

The Asuras replied, "Oh great BrahmaDev, since we cannot be immortal and invincible, we ask for a safe haven to protect us from the attacks of our enemies. Please build us three fortresses, glorious, prosperous, and luxurious, that will be invulnerable to any invasion by the Devas. Let one be made of gold, another of silver, and the third of iron. We will reside in these fortresses and travel freely between them. They must be impregnable and everlasting. As a condition for their destruction, let them be vulnerable only to a single, extraordinary arrow shot by Lord Shiva from a magnificent chariot."

The Asuras believed that Lord Shiva, being their revered deity, would never attack them. Moreover, they thought it highly unlikely that Shiva could destroy all three fortresses with a single arrow. BrahmaDev replied, "Mighty Asuras, I will grant your wish immediately."

Without delay, Brahma summoned Maya, the renowned architect of the Asuras, and instructed him, "Mayasura, build three fortified cities for them. One of gold, one of silver, and one of iron. Use whatever resources you need."

Following Brahma's instructions, Mayasura built the three cities. The golden city was constructed in the heavens, the silver city in the sky, and the iron city on the earth. The cities were distributed among the three brothers, and the Asuras took control of them. These cities became sanctuaries for Asuras from across the world, who flocked to Tripura to live. The fortresses were mobile and could travel wherever the Asuras desired. However, they would only align in a straight line once every thousand years, during the conjunction of the star Pushya with the moon.

The cities were lavishly adorned with Kalpavrikshas, elephants, horses, and fountains. Radiant like the sun, they boasted towering skyscrapers and Shiva temples. The cities were also home to Yaga platforms, monuments, gardens, parks, rivers, forests, universities, stadiums, and wildlife sanctuaries. The Asuras lived happily, without harming others, and were free from the disturbances of the Devas and other adversaries.

Unfortunately, after years of peace, the Asuras' inherent evil nature resurfaced. They began to tyrannize and torment the Devas. While Mayasura continued his worship of Shiva, the rest of the Asuras launched attacks on the Devas, shattering the peace of the worlds.

The Devas were overcome with immense grief as the Asuras overwhelmed them. Indra and the rest of the Devas, filled with dejection, approached Lord Brahma for help.

They said, "Dear BrahmaDev, the sons of Taraka have become invincible due to your blessings. Now, they are tormenting us, and we can no longer bear their oppression. Since you are responsible for granting them this power, we ask that you provide a solution once and for all."

BrahmaDev replied, "Dear Devas, please calm down. It is true that I made them invincible, but they have become far more powerful than I anticipated. I cannot defeat them on my own. We must seek Lord Shiva's help, as he is the only one capable of assisting us."

Following Brahma's suggestion, the Devas went to Mount Kailasa to meet Lord Shiva. Upon seeing his guests, Shiva said, "Devas, it seems something terrible has befallen you. Tell me what troubles you."

They replied, "Almighty Lord Shiva, your devotees, Tarakaksha, Vidyunmali, and Kamalaksha, have become empowered by BrahmaDev's boon and are now torturing us. They have unleashed their malevolent behaviour upon all forms of life in the universe. If they continue, it will lead to our doom. Please help us."

Shiva responded, "My dear Devas, I cannot attack the Asuras right now. From what you have said, and from what I perceive, the Puras are home to numerous temples and universities that promote devotion and the sciences. The Asuras are deeply committed to their worship, performing Yagas and Pujas in their temples. They are not acting against Dharma, as far as I can sense. How can I destroy them under these circumstances? If you need help, you must seek Lord Vishnu."

After hearing Shiva's words, the Devas, along with BrahmaDev, went to Lord Vishnu and informed him of their dire situation.

Vishnu said, "BrahmaDev, Devas, where Dharma prevails, grief cannot endure. It disappears just as darkness vanishes in the presence of sunlight."

The Devas, disappointed by Vishnu's response, pondered their situation. Until now, they had always regarded Vishnu as their saviour in difficult times, but it seemed as though he had abandoned them. Unable to contain their grief any longer, they said, "Vishnu Deva, your philosophies will not save us from the Asuras. As long as Tripura exists, there will be no Dharma. Destroy the Puras if you can; otherwise, you will witness the downfall of the Devas with your own eyes."

Vishnu sensed the deep sorrow and distress of the Devas. After contemplating for a moment, he thought, "How can I destroy the devotees of Shiva?" Immediately, he created countless giant beasts and said, "Devas, do not worry. These beasts will destroy the Puras for us."

Relieved by Vishnu's words, the Devas left with hope.

Vishnu then sent the beasts to attack the Puras. However, as soon as they approached one of the Puras, they were incinerated by its radiating light. One by one, Vishnu's beasts were burned to ashes. Those that survived returned to Vishnu to recount their failure.

Vishnu realized, "The three Puras are fortified by the power of Shiva's blessings and the severe penances of the Asuras. They are invulnerable. It is nearly impossible to destroy them. The only way to defeat the Asuras is to divert them from their Dharmic path and devotion."

Determined to find a solution, Vishnu immersed himself in deep thought. Finally, he devised a plan. He created a man of unparalleled brilliance. A sage with a shaved head, dressed in torn clothes, and holding a broom in one hand. Bowing to Vishnu, the sage asked, "What is my duty? What should I do? What is my name?"

Vishnu replied, "You shall be known as Ariha. With your sharp and cunning mind, you will perform great acts of Maya. Your task is to visit the inhabitants of the three Puras and, with the power of illusion, lead them astray from their Dharmic values and devotion. This will bring about their destruction. Afterward, you shall reside in the desert on Earth and remain there until the end of Kali Yuga."

With Vishnu's blessings, Ariha set off to fulfil his mission.

Without delay, Ariha created four disciples and taught them the science and art of Maya. Clad in torn clothes and carrying brooms, Ariha and his disciples roamed through the Puras, spreading their teachings. However, due to the strength of Shiva's blessings, neither Ariha nor his disciples could influence the inhabitants of Tripura.

Ariha informed Vishnu of the situation, and Vishnu immediately summoned Narada. When Narada arrived, he asked, "O Vishnu Deva, why have you called me? Tell me what you need."

Vishnu replied, "Dear Sage Narada, you must be aware of the recent developments concerning the sons of Tarakasura and their stronghold, Tripura. We need to destroy it to ensure the safety of the Deva clan. I have already sent Ariha and his disciples to divert the Asuras from their Dharma, but their powers have proven ineffective. Only you can help us now."

Narada smiled and agreed. He set out for Tripura.

The Asuras of Tripura welcomed Narada with open arms, as he was a renowned sage. Narada said to them, "O Asuras, your Tripura is truly magnificent. But I have come here to meet a well-known Maharshi and his disciples, who, I have heard, now reside here. Their glory is unparalleled. I consider myself fortunate to have the chance to receive alms from them. You should do the same, for it will bring you tremendous prosperity and wealth. You may never get such an opportunity again."

Trusting Narada's words, the Asuras visited Ariha and his disciples, who were wandering through Tripura. As soon as the Asuras received alms from them, they lost sight of their penances and Dharmic values. They became consumed by lust and desires, abandoning their Yagas and Shiva Pujas. They began to treat the women among them as mere possessions, reducing them to objects of pleasure. Tripura quickly descended into a hub of Adharmic activities.

Soon after, the Devas, along with Vishnu and Brahma, rushed to Mount Kailasa to meet Lord Shiva. They pleaded, "Dear Lord Shiva, Almighty God, Supreme Being, the Asuras have forsaken their Dharmic values and have even abandoned their routine Shiva Pujas. They are tormenting humans and Devas alike. If this continues, both Devas and humans will face extinction. We beg you to save us by destroying the Asuras."

Shiva replied, "Devas, Vishnu, and BrahmaDev, I am fully aware of your suffering. The Asuras have indeed chosen the path of Adharma, and I can no longer tolerate it. For this reason, I will destroy their fortresses and annihilate them. Rest assured, there is no doubt about this. But I have one question: If Vishnu was able to divert the Asuras from their Dharmic path, why could you not solve this problem on your own?"

Vishnu, embarrassed by Shiva's words, remained silent. BrahmaDev intervened, "O Lord, Vishnu and I were born from you. Thus, we do not possess your power or abilities. Moreover, you are responsible for the protection of your devotees and the Devas. You alone have the authority to punish the wicked and bless the virtuous. It is time to put an end to the most malevolent beings in the universe. This task falls within your jurisdiction, and only you have the power to destroy Tripura."

Shiva replied, "Very well, I agree. I will destroy Tripura and the Asuras. But I cannot do it alone. This must be a combined effort by the Devas, as I lack the necessary resources to carry out the task. If you can provide what I require, I will construct a chariot and a weapon to bring down Tripura."

Brahma said, "Mighty Lord, just tell us what to bring."

Following Shiva's instructions, a grand war chariot was

constructed. The earth itself became the chariot, with the Sun and Moon serving as its wheels. Brahma held the reins. Mount Meru became the bow, and the serpent Shesha served as the bowstring. Vishnu transformed into the arrow, while Agni, the God of Fire, became the tip of the arrow. Vayu, the God of Air, became the feathers at the rear of the arrow. All the other Devas assumed their respective roles and forms within the chariot, while the four Vedas became the horses.

Lord Shiva mounted the chariot and drove it towards Tripura. However, as Shiva prepared for battle, the divine chariot would not move forward. Sensing this, Vishnu transformed into a bull and pushed the chariot to give it the necessary momentum. Coincidentally, at that moment, the three Puras aligned, an event that only occurs once every thousand years. As the fortified cities aligned, Shiva readied himself to string the mighty bow. The Devas were overjoyed, believing that Tripura would be destroyed due to their efforts.

But Shiva did not fire the arrow. Instead, he smiled, sensing the arrogance of the Devas, which he found somewhat insulting. Suddenly, all three Puras began to burn on their own. Surprised by this, Brahma turned to the Devas and said, "Devas, cast aside your pride immediately. We had nothing to do with the destruction of Tripura. Look for yourselves. Lord Shiva has burned Tripura without any help from us."

The Devas immediately apologized. BrahmaDev then requested, "Dear Lord Shiva, please forgive the Devas and release the arrow. Otherwise, the Devas will be left with a never-ending bad reputation. Moreover, the entire effort of building the chariot will have been in vain."

At Brahma's request, Shiva fired the arrow at the already burning Puras. In an instant, the three fortified cities crumbled into dust and ashes.

The Devas said, "O Lord Shiva, Almighty God, we have come to understand the truth of your power. Even though the prophecy said, 'One arrow, one shot, and the Puras will be destroyed,' it is you who holds the ultimate power over all."

Aware of his innocent devotee, Mayasura, the architect of the Puras, Shiva had sent Nandi before the battle to warn him. Informed of the impending destruction, Mayasura fled Tripura, abandoning the great city he had built. After destroying Tripura, Lord Shiva acquired the name *Tripuranthaka*, meaning "The Destroyer of Tripura."

19

AGNI

In ancient times, there lived a Rishi named Vishwanana in the city of Narmapura, near the banks of the river Narmada. Vishwanana was known for his kind and righteous nature, and he was a devoted follower of Lord Shiva. His wife, Shichishmati, was also praised for her exemplary conduct.

Vishwanana led a life of selfless devotion, committed to pujas and meditation. One day, Shichishmati approached her husband and said, "Beloved, I am deeply grateful to have you as my husband. I have no complaints and look forward to spending the rest of my life with you. Yet, I have one wish that I would like you to fulfill: I ask that we have a son who embodies the spirit of Lord Shiva."

Vishwanana replied, "Dear wife, you have been a loyal companion all your life, and I could ask for nothing more. Therefore, I will travel to Kashi and begin a penance in hopes that Lord Shiva will grant us this boon."

Vishwanana then journeyed to Kashi and began his meditation on the banks of the holy river Ganga. He spent years in deep penance until, one day, Lord Shiva appeared before him.

Lord Shiva asked, "Vishwanana, I have observed your strict penance. Why do you seek me?"

Vishwanana bowed and replied, "I bow to you, Almighty Lord, the omniscient and omnipotent. You bring joy and sanctity to your devoted followers. There is no wish I could have that is hidden from your all-knowing wisdom. Please grant me a boon that you deem I am worthy of."

Lord Shiva smiled and said, "My dear disciple, tell your wife that her wish will soon be fulfilled. I will be born as your son. My incarnation will be known as Grihapati, and he will be a divine figure worshipped by mortals."

Vishwanana returned home with the joyful news, and his wife, Shichishmati, who had been anxiously awaiting his return, was overjoyed. Soon after, Shichishmati became pregnant, and after eight months, she gave birth to a baby boy.

As the child was born, flowers bloomed across the three worlds. Many prominent Rishis, scholars, and Devas visited the child to celebrate his birth. BrahmaDev himself offered to write the child's horoscope and named him Grihapati. The Devas, including BrahmaDev and Vishnu, blessed Grihapati before returning to their respective abodes.

On Grihapati's ninth birthday, the sage Narada visited him and performed a palm reading to predict his future.

Narada summoned Grihapati's parents and said, "Grihapati will be worshipped by many, and he will live a glorious life. However, there is one problem. When he reaches the age of twelve, he is destined to die, struck by lightning. Only Lord Shiva can help him."

Vishwanana and Shichishmati were horrified upon hearing this, feeling as though their world had crumbled. They wept in despair, fearing for their son's life.

Trying to console them, Grihapati said, "Mother, Father, do not weep. There is no need to despair. Death cannot conquer me. As long as I am your son, Yama will not take me. A lightning strike will not end my life. From this moment, I will begin praying to Lord Shiva."

Hearing these words, his parents were reassured, and Grihapati left to begin his deep devotion to Lord Shiva.

For years, Grihapati performed intense penance until he reached the age of twelve. Then, one day, IndraDev appeared before him and said, "O Brahmin boy, I am Indra, King of the Devas and God of Thunder. I am pleased with your devotion. Ask for any boon, and I will grant it to you."

Grihapati, angered, replied, "I have never prayed to you. I worship only Lord Shiva. I do not need your blessings or boons. Leave me in peace to continue my devotion to Lord Shiva."

IndraDev responded, "O child, Shiva is a weak god. I, Indra, am the mightiest of all gods. There is no wish that I cannot fulfil. Instead of wasting your time worshipping Shiva, you should worship me. Ask me for anything you desire."

Enraged, Grihapati shouted, "You arrogant fool! I know your true nature. You are the most conceited among the Devas, and you exploit the innocent. I will never ask for anything from you. I worship only Lord Shiva. Now leave at once!"

Indra, furious, raised his thunderbolt and aimed it at Grihapati.

He said, "I will strike you down now. If you ask for forgiveness and renounce Shiva, I may spare you."

Grihapati stood firm, closed his eyes, and shouted, "If you want to kill me for worshipping Shiva, then so be it!"

Suddenly, Grihapati felt a gentle hand on his shoulder. He opened his eyes to see Lord Shiva standing before him, resplendent in all his glory.

Shiva smiled and said, "Dear child, you no longer need to fear Indra, nor do you need to fear Yama. No one can harm you. It was I who came in disguise as Indra to test your devotion, and you have passed. As a reward, I bless you. From this moment, you will take on the role of Agni, the god of fire, and you will be one of the Devas. People will worship you."

The Shivalinga that Grihapati, now Agni, established became known as Agneeswara and has since remained a sacred deity for worship.

20

HANUMAN

Once, there was an Apsaras named Punchikasthala, who lived in Brihaspati's ashram in Devaloka. One day, a group of Gandharvas was undergoing physical training nearby. Punchikasthala, distracted, forgot her duties at the ashram and began gazing at the Gandharvas with lust. Noticing her absence, Brihaspati found her staring at the Gandharvas, neglecting her responsibilities. Furious, Brihaspati confronted her and shouted, "How dare you stand here gawking at the Gandharvas while abandoning your duties in the ashram?"

Humiliated, Punchikasthala replied, "Why do you care? Are you jealous? Does it bother you that I am not interested in you in the same way?"

Brihaspati was enraged. Even the Devas feared to insult him in such a manner. He angrily shouted, "I curse you! You shall be transformed into a monkey!"

Realizing her mistake, Punchikasthala pleaded, "Oh Rishi, I have committed a grave error. Please forgive me and undo the curse."

Brihaspati calmed down and said, "You will be freed from the curse when you give birth to an avatar of Lord Shiva."

As foretold, Punchikasthala was born as the Vanara Anjana on Earth. Upon her birth in a jungle, she felt extremely hungry and went in search of food. After wandering through the forest, she came upon a mango tree. Without hesitation, she leaped up to a branch and grabbed a mango. Suddenly, she heard a loud roar.

Startled, Anjana looked around and saw a giant Rakshasa emerge from the trees. The Rakshasa approached her and said, "Hey beautiful ape! Why are you here alone?"

"Please don't harm me. Leave me alone," Anjana replied, terrified.

"Why would I harm you? I am captivated by your beauty. I am Shambasadana, king of this jungle. Come with me and be my consort!"

"No! I can't!" Anjana screamed and ran away.

The Rakshasa chased her. After a long, exhausting sprint, Anjana reached an ashram. Confused and frightened, she sought refuge among the Rishis, who quickly came to her aid.

"Who are you? Why were you running?" they asked.

"Respected Rishis, I am Anjana. A Rakshasa named Shambasadana is chasing me. Please help me," she begged.

"Do not worry, child," one of the Rishis reassured her. "We will summon someone to protect you."

Soon, a valiant and muscular Vanara named Veerkesari arrived. He consoled Anjana, saying, "Do not worry. I will protect you."

Not long after, Shambasadana arrived at the ashram and shouted, "Hey monkey girl! You think you can hide here among these weak humans? I will drag you back to my dwelling whether you like it or not!"

Veerkesari stepped in front of the Rakshasa, shielding Anjana from his sight. "You will have to get through me first," Veerkesari declared. "Only then can you lay a finger on her."

"A fight it is, then!" the Rakshasa roared, lunging at Veerkesari.

A fierce battle ensued, with neither gaining the upper hand. They were equally matched. Desperate, Anjana prayed to Lord Shiva, "Dear Lord, help Veerkesari defeat Shambasadana. Please show me a way."

An inner voice answered, "Anjana, Shambasadana can only be killed by a blow from his own blood."

Anjana quickly grabbed a sabre that had fallen from Shambasadana and dipped it in his blood. She then handed it to Veerkesari, shouting, "Use this to kill him!"

Immediately, Veerkesari stabbed Shambasadana with the blood-soaked sabre. The once-dominant Rakshasa collapsed and took his last breath. Overcome with gratitude for her rescue, Anjana expressed her deep affection for Veerkesari, who had never felt happier. The Rishis of the ashram soon conducted the marriage ceremony of Veerkesari and Anjana.

Years passed, but the couple remained childless, which saddened Anjana. She pleaded with her husband, "Beloved, we need a child. If we begin praying to Lord Shiva, perhaps he will bless us."

Thus, Anjana and Veerkesari began their penance to Lord Shiva. Meanwhile, on Mount Kailash, Shiva and Parvati noticed the Vanara couple's devotion.

"What do they seek, dear husband?" Parvati asked. "What do they want in return for their deep meditation?"

Shiva replied, "Anjana bears a curse that can only be broken with the birth of my avatar from her. It is time to fulfil the prophecy."

Shiva then summoned Vayudev, the wind god, and gave him an embryo. "Implant this in Anjana. The child born to her will be my avatar on Earth."

As instructed by Shiva, Vayudev travelled to the meditating couple and implanted the divine embryo in Anjana. Sensing that their prayers had been answered, Anjana shared the joyful news with her husband. The couple was elated, certain that their child would be the avatar of Lord Shiva.

Upon hearing the news from Rishi Narada, Bali, the king of the Vanaras, grew anxious. Concerned that a Vanara with the power of Shiva might overshadow him, Bali tried to prevent the child's birth by pouring scorching Panchaloha over Anjana's embryo while she slept. However, the attempt failed. Instead, when the child was born, he had earrings made of Panchaloha. As soon as the child came into the world, Anjana was freed from her curse.

The child, Hanuman, grew up learning the Vedas from Surya, the Sun God. As a token of gratitude, he vowed to help Surya's son, Sugreeva. With the blessings of Vayudev and Veerkesari, Hanuman set off for Kishkinda, the Vanara kingdom where Sugreeva had been banished. Hanuman became Sugreeva's close ally until he met Rama, who was searching for his wife, Sita, after she had been abducted by the Asura king Ravana. With Rama's help, Hanuman aided Sugreeva in defeating the wicked Bali and installing Sugreeva as the king of Kishkinda.

As agreed, Sugreeva dispatched the Vanara army to help Rama find and rescue Sita from Ravana's hold. Hanuman dedicated his life to this cause, becoming the most devoted follower of Rama.

21

PANDAVA'S PAST LIVES

Once upon a time, the Devas conducted a grand Yaga in the Naimisha Forest, with Yama Dev as the chief host. As Yama was fully absorbed in the rituals of the Yaga, he neglected his duties of collecting souls from Earth. Consequently, no living beings died, and creatures began living immortally, throwing the world out of balance. Alarmed, the Devas approached Brahma and explained the dire situation.

Brahma calmly replied, "Do not worry, Devas. The Yaga will conclude soon, and Yama will resume his duties."

Reassured by Brahma's words, the Devas returned to the Yaga, which was nearing its conclusion by the banks of the Ganga River. As they watched the Yaga platform, their attention was suddenly drawn elsewhere. A stunningly beautiful young woman appeared, holding a pot in her hand. The Devas were mesmerized by her beauty, and Indra Dev was especially captivated.

The young woman began to shed tears, and as each tear fell into the Ganga, it transformed into a lotus flower. Indra, curious and intrigued, observed this magical sight. The other Devas remarked, "This is no ordinary woman. Her grief must be extraordinary. Shouldn't we do something to comfort her?"

Indra approached her, but as he neared, she walked further toward the source of the Ganga. He called out, "Lady, who are you? Why do you weep? Tell me the cause of your sorrow, and I will solve your problem."

The woman, however, ignored Indra and continued walking. Confused and curious, Indra thought, "Who is this woman? Why is she ignoring me? Is she mute? She doesn't seem to be royalty, nor an Apsara, nor the wife of any Deva or Asura. I must uncover her identity."

Determined, Indra followed her through a valley and along the edges of the mountains until he finally reached the source of the Ganga. However, the mysterious woman had vanished, and instead, he found himself in the presence of Lord Shiva and Goddess Parvati. The woman was nowhere to be seen, and Indra began to panic.

Just as he was about to leave, Shiva called out, "Indra, where are you running off to?"

Indra froze in shock, believing that Shiva hadn't noticed him. Trembling, he turned back to face the god.

Shiva continued, "Why did you ignore me and run away? If your intention was to insult me, why come all the way here?"

Indra, terrified, couldn't conceal the truth any longer. He feared how Shiva might react to his desire-driven pursuit. Shiva pressed further, "Why are you silent? Who sent you here?"

Realizing he had no choice, Indra confessed, "Lord Shiva, I was following a beautiful young woman. I saw her at the Yaga in the Naimisha Forest. She was mysterious, and I wanted to know who she was. That's why I followed her here, but she suddenly vanished, and now I cannot find her."

Shiva smiled knowingly and said, "Ah, so that's the reason. I expected this to happen. There's no need to worry. Do you see that large cave over there?" He pointed toward a nearby cave. "Go there, and you will find what you seek."

Following Shiva's instructions, Indra approached the cave, which was blocked by a huge boulder. After much effort, he managed to move the boulder and enter the cave. To his astonishment, he found four other Indras inside. He was stunned and couldn't comprehend what he was seeing.

Shiva appeared beside him and explained, "Indra, do not be alarmed. These are Indras, just like you. They are Vishwabhuk, Bhoothadhamavu, Shibi, and Shanti. You are merely one among them. There have been many Indras before you, and there will be many more after you. The position of Indra is a role, a title held by the one who rules Devaloka. The young woman you followed was Sri Devi. All five of you were captivated by her charm, and as a result, she will marry all of you." With these words, Lord Shiva disappeared.

The five Indras, confused and humbled, went to Lord Vishnu and prayed for guidance. Lord Vishnu appeared and said, "Each of you was Indra in a different era, representing different times. You ruled the heavens without knowing one another. Time itself is a boundary that no one can cross. Indras, you are simply points in the continuum of time. As the ages pass, more Indras will come. However, you all desired Sri Devi, and now you must face the consequences of that materialistic desire. You will be born as humans on Earth, and Sri Devi will be your wife, but you will experience the sorrows and challenges of mortal life. Only by enduring these earthly struggles will you attain Moksha. Do not worry, though, I will also be born on Earth to help and guide you."

Thus, the five Indras were born on Earth as the five Pandava brothers, and Sri Devi was born as Panchali. Lord Vishnu incarnated as Krishna, and he helped guide the Pandavas through their trials and tribulations.

22

KIRATA AVATAR

Duryodhana and the Kauravas defeated the mighty Pandavas in a deceitful gamble, forcing the Pandavas and their wife, Panchali, into exile in the Dwaita Forest after they abdicated their throne. Though they led adventurous lives in the forest, the Pandavas were disheartened and depressed, knowing that their enemies ruled their kingdom.

Krishna frequently came to their aid. One day, sensing the distress of the Pandavas and Panchali, he said, "My dear friends, do not worry. Once your period of exile is over, you will reclaim your rightful kingdom from the Kauravas."

Yudhishthira, the wisest of the Pandavas, responded, "But the Kauravas have a vast army and hold the upper hand. We will need divine support to be victorious."

Krishna declared, "The Almighty Lord Shiva is the destroyer of evil and sorrow. He blesses all who worship him. You must all devote yourselves to him. Lord Shiva is the most powerful god, maintaining the balance of the universe. This is the absolute truth. Believe me, those who seek freedom and grace must serve Lord Shiva. He is the supreme god, the destroyer of the wicked, and a beacon of hope for all. However, Lord Shiva is known for testing his devotees. The strongest among you must undertake penance to earn his blessings."

Yudhishthira replied, "Krishna, we are grateful for your guidance. This is the solution to all our problems. Among us, none is more qualified than Arjuna to perform penance and seek Lord Shiva's favour."

Soon after, Maharshi Vyasa arrived and imparted lessons on Shakravidya to Arjuna. He said, "Arjuna, you must journey to the sacred Mount Indrakila in the Himalayas. It is a peaceful abode for many sages who engage in prayers and strict penances. The Shakravidya will be of great benefit to you."

With Vyasa's blessings, Arjuna set off for Mount Indrakila. Once there, he chose a secluded spot and fashioned a Shivaling from mud to perform severe penance to Lord Shiva. As he began his worship, a radiant halo appeared behind him, illuminating the surrounding area. Arjuna continued his penance without pause. Though the rest of the Pandavas and Panchali missed him deeply, they bore their grief for the sake of their greater cause.

A messenger of Indra, witnessing the scene, hurried back to Devaloka and reported, "IndraDev, I saw a strange but divine young man performing intense penance on Mount Indrakila. He is radiating tremendous heat. You must do something."

Realizing that the young man was none other than his son, Arjuna, Indra was concerned that the penance might be so severe it could lead to Arjuna's death. Disguised as an old Brahmin, Indra descended to Arjuna's meditation spot.

Seeing the Brahmin approach, Arjuna respectfully greeted him and asked, "Who are you, Brahmin, and what brings you here?"

The old Brahmin said, "Young man, I can see you are devout, but you must stop this penance. It will lead to nothing. The path you are on is a waste of time."

Arjuna replied, "Brahmin, I have served you as a guest, but you have no right to interrupt my worship. Whatever you say, I will continue to honour the Almighty Lord Shiva."

Realizing Arjuna's resolve, Indra revealed his true form. Arjuna bowed down to him.

Indra said, "My son, I am proud of you. Your devotion is unwavering, and Lord Shiva will surely bless you. Your wish will be granted. But remember, once you regain your throne, rule justly and avoid the path of Adharma."

Indra blessed Arjuna and returned to Devaloka. Arjuna resumed his penance, and his growing radiance caught the attention of the Devas. Concerned, they approached Lord Shiva, who was sitting beside Parvati, and asked him to intervene. Lord Shiva smiled and assured them, "I am aware of the situation. I will handle it. Do not worry."

After the Devas left, Parvati asked, "You've been aware of Arjuna's penance all this time, yet you haven't blessed him. Are you planning something, my lord?"

Shiva replied, "Arjuna needs a weapon for the upcoming war. I must ensure that he is worthy and will use it wisely. I am testing his commitment."

Meanwhile, Duryodhana learned that Arjuna was performing severe penance to please Lord Shiva. Fearing that Arjuna might receive a powerful weapon, Duryodhana approached Muka, a malicious Asura, and said, "Muka, a warrior of your power deserves better than this humble existence. Help me, and I will reward you with a life of luxury in my palace."

Muka agreed eagerly. Duryodhana added, "But remember, Arjuna must not know that I sent you. This mission must remain secret. You will need to disguise yourself."

Muka replied, "Don't worry. I will transform into a wild boar and attack him. The world will believe that Arjuna was killed by a mere animal."

Muka arrived at Mount Indrakila and transformed himself into a wild boar. He charged toward the meditating Arjuna, uprooting trees, shattering boulders, and making loud noises along the way. The boar raced to the spot where Arjuna was performing his penance. Sensing the boar's presence, Arjuna opened his eyes and thought, "This is no ordinary boar. I can feel it. Who is it? Where does it come from? What is its intention? On whose orders is it acting? This is a formidable demon, and I'm certain its primary goal is to disrupt my penance. One can discern the nature of a being by its behaviour, knowledge by its words, and love by its eyes. The mind of a being can be assessed through its movements, form, emotions, and deeds. By this understanding, I can deduce that this boar has come to kill me. Therefore, it is my enemy, and I shall annihilate it."

At that moment, Lord Shiva arrived, disguised as a *Kirata* chief, accompanied by his Shivaganas, who were also disguised as Kirata warriors. Observing the boar charging toward Arjuna, Shiva recognized it as the Asura Muka, intent on killing Arjuna. To thwart this threat, the Kirata chief shot multiple arrows at the boar, while Arjuna simultaneously aimed his own arrows. As the arrows struck, the animal reverted to its original Asura form and fell dead.

Seeing the boar transform into an Asura upon its death, Arjuna thought, "I was right; this was indeed a demon."

Arjuna approached the slain Asura to retrieve his arrows but was joined by a Kirata hunter sent by the chief. Ignoring the hunter, Arjuna took an arrow from the Asura's body.

The Kirata hunter shouted, "What nonsense are you committing? That arrow belongs to us! Drop it and leave!"

Arjuna replied, "Foolish hunter, end your arrogance at once. I shot this arrow, and there is no one in the world who can rival my marksmanship. How can this be yours? If you desire it so badly, I can donate it to you, but do not claim it as your own."

The hunter retorted, "You seem like a person engaged in penance. How can you lie so blatantly while being a devotee? Did you think you could leave here through deceit? Our chief is here with us. The boar was shot down by him to save you. If you want the arrows, ask our chief; he will give them to you. He might even provide you with more if you need."

Enraged, Arjuna yelled, "You foolish hunter! I do not wish to fight you. Call your chief! I will show him who I am. Call him quickly!"

The hunters informed their chief of the situation, and the Kirata chief appeared before Arjuna. Fearing a battle, Arjuna readied his bow and arrow for attack.

The Kirata chief said, "Young man, take a good look at my warriors. Do you truly believe you could win a battle against us? You should run away before matters escalate. You need not sacrifice your life over such a minor issue. Your brothers might be waiting for your return. Do you not wish to see them again?"

Arjuna replied furiously, "Although this is a minor issue, if I surrender to you, I will be forsaking my Kshatriya Dharma. My brothers and mother will grieve if I do so. All that I have learned will be in vain. Therefore, we shall settle this through combat."

The battle commenced. To Arjuna's shock, the Kirata chief dominated the fight, completely overpowering him. Closing his eyes, Arjuna prayed to Lord Shiva for strength. He managed to land a punch on the Kirata chief for the first time. Yet, surprisingly, the chief laughed. Arjuna stared at him in astonishment.

In a moment of revelation, the Kirata chief transformed back into Lord Shiva, and all the Kirata hunters morphed into the Shivaganas.

Realizing it was Lord Shiva in disguise, Arjuna touched his feet and said, "Oh dear Lord! I have awaited this moment for many years. You have blessed me by revealing yourself. Your form is divine. I am ashamed I did not recognize you in your disguise; your power of Maya has truly overwhelmed me."

Arjuna continued, "God of all, Supreme God! Please forgive me for my actions. I behaved poorly without recognizing who you were. I apologize; I did not know you were testing me. I was a fool to challenge you to a battle. Oh, Almighty God, please bless me."

Lord Shiva replied, "Arjuna, I know you are my devoted follower. Do not delve on what you have done. I orchestrated this to test you. Do not be sad." He then lifted Arjuna with both hands. "You are the mightiest of the Pandavas. I consider the punch you delivered as part of your trial. I anticipated that. You may ask for anything you desire, and I will gladly grant it."

With tears in his eyes, Arjuna replied, "All-forgiving God! You are the only hope for the world. It is beyond my ability to express your greatness. I bow to you in respect. Almighty Lord Shiva, please protect me from the dangers posed by my enemies."

Upon hearing Arjuna's request, Lord Shiva gifted him with the Pashupata, an unparalleled weapon from his armoury. "Dear Arjuna, use this weapon when the time comes. It is unrivalled, and you will be invincible. I have appointed Krishna to assist you whenever you need. Krishna is one of my best devotees, and he serves me well. You can trust him. I bless you to reclaim your throne and to rule wisely with your brothers, in accordance with Dharma."

With Lord Shiva's blessings, Arjuna returned to the Pandava settlement in the forest, where he shared his experience with his brothers. Filled with joy, they praised Lord Shiva and felt confident that their destiny would be glorious.

With the Pashupata, Arjuna was able to defeat Karna in the inevitable Mahabharata War at Kurukshetra.

23

OUTSET OF SHIVALAYOTTAM

Shivalayaottam is a traditional celebration performed by Hindus in Kerala and Tamil Nadu during Shivaratri. Devotees visit twelve Shiva temples in the Kanyakumari district of South India. These temples are Tirumala, Tikkurissi, Triparappu, Tirunanthikara, Tiruponmana, Tripannipakam, Tiruneelakandam, Tirumelakodu, Tiruvidaykodu, Tiruvithamkodu, Tripannikodu, and Tirunattalam. There is an interesting story behind Shivalayaottam that dates back to the Mahabharata period in Dwapara Yuga.

It all began when the Pandavas decided to arrange a Yaga in

their sacred yard. Yudhishthira, being the eldest, invited all the rishis of the kingdom, including the Shiva devotee Maharshi Vyakrapada. However, he ignored the invitation.

Upon learning this, Bhima felt humiliated and consulted Lord Krishna. "I don't understand why Maharshi Vyakrapada ignored our invitation to the Yaga. It is truly disgraceful. It's not just a matter of including every sage in the kingdom; it is also about our honour. Please give me a solution to this problem."

Lord Krishna replied, "Dear Bhima, you claim to be the strongest person on earth, yet you are upset that a frail old sage is ignoring you. If you try, you can surely bring him to the Yaga."

Listening to Krishna, Bhima thought it would be an easy task, unaware of Vyakrapada's true power. When he visited Vyakrapada's ashram, he found the sage deep in meditation. An irritated Bhima yelled, "Hey, Maharshi! Wake up! Wake up!" But the rishi did not stir. Bhima continued his loud interruptions until he suddenly felt a searing sensation. He realized this was Vyakrapada's supernatural power. Afraid and unsure of what to do, Bhima fled back to Krishna.

"Krishna," he said, "Vyakrapada will certainly harm me with his powers. I can't handle that old man!"

Krishna replied, "How is it that the strongest man on earth is confused about completing a simple task? You can solve this problem yourself. In any case, I will help you." Krishna handed Bhima twelve Shivalingas and instructed, "Use these appropriately."

Once again, Bhima entered Vyakrapada's ashram and disturbed his meditation. This time, Vyakrapada became furious and threatened to chase Bhima down. "You ignorant fool! When I catch you, I will curse you to walk on your hands and eat with your nose!"

Bhima started running. When he became exhausted, he set down a Shivalinga. Being a staunch devotee of Lord Shiva,

Vyakrapada forgot about Bhima and began performing puja on the Shivalinga. Bhima used this opportunity to catch his breath. When Vyakrapada finished his prayers, Bhima resumed his flight. When he grew tired again, he placed down the second Shivalinga, and Vyakrapada began his puja on that one too. This continued until Bhima ran out of Shivalingas, with Vyakrapada close to catching him. Just then, Lord Vishnu and Lord Shiva appeared as one.

In that moment, Bhima realized that his God Vishnu is also Shiva, and Vyakrapada understood that Shiva is Vishnu. Both Bhima and Rishi Vyakrapada recognized that all gods are one. Vyakrapada forgave Bhima and agreed to attend the Yaga.

Legends say that the Shivalingas present at those twelve temples are the ones placed by Bhima. Additionally, near the twelfth temple, there is a Vishnu temple, symbolizing his appearance with Lord Shiva at the last moment.

(24)

SOMNATH

Before the birth of Sati, Daksha had twenty-seven daughters. Chandra, the moon god, married all twenty-seven of them. With Chandra's presence, they became even more beautiful. However, among the wives, Chandra loved Rohini the most because of her unparalleled beauty. He began to spend all his time with Rohini, which made the other wives feel terrible. They were devastated by the lack of affection from their husband.

One day, the wives shared their grief with their father, Daksha. Unhappy about the situation, Daksha approached Chandra and calmly said, "Dear son, you are my favourite among the Devas. You should bring happiness to all who depend on you. Is it right to make your wives sorrowful? Aren't they all equal to you? Why are you ignoring the rest of your wives while directing all your affection to Rohini? This is a sin. Therefore, you must not repeat this behaviour."

Daksha returned, believing that his son-in-law would obey him. However, Chandra continued his affection for Rohini while neglecting his other wives.

Upon learning that Chandra had not followed his request, Daksha felt annoyed. He was infuriated that twenty-six of his daughters were upset and suffering. Daksha went to Chandra once again, attempting to advise him while suppressing his anger. When he realized that Chandra was arrogant and impossible to change, he cursed him, saying, "You egotistical Deva, I tried to warn you many times not to show favouritism. But you arrogantly ignored my words. You shall pay for your disobedience. Your body will begin to decay to nothingness from now on."

Chandra was shocked by the curse, and its effects became apparent immediately. His body decayed day by day; he grew weak and fell apart. The *Maharshis* on earth felt the alarming situation. Without Chandra, the balance of the earth would be in peril. They panicked. Chandra shared his worries with Indra and the other Devas. Along with the Rishis and Devas, Chandra went to BrahmaDev and requested help.

BrahmaDev replied, "Dear Devas and Rishis, there is no need to worry. Chandra has received a befitting punishment. Let's hope he reflects on his mistakes. However, once a curse is in effect, it cannot be retracted. But I have a solution: take Chandra to earth and establish a Shivalinga there. Chandra should begin his penance to please Lord Shiva by worshipping the Shivalinga. Shiva will surely help you with this problem."

Listening to Brahma's advice, Chandra, along with the Devas and Rishis, established a Shivalinga on earth and began praying to Shiva. Recognizing Chandra's earnest devotion, Lord Shiva appeared before him and asked, "Chandra Dev, blessings! What do you seek? I will grant your wish."

Chandra replied, "Dear Lord, can't you see I am suffering from decay? My body crumbles more each day, and I will die within days. Please help me escape this curse. I realize the mistakes I have made and ask for forgiveness."

Shiva said, "Chandra, I am aware of your misery. A curse once given cannot be revoked. But don't worry; I can help you. As your body continues to disintegrate, you will regain your form and power in subsequent days. This cycle will continue, and you shall have no end."

Lord Shiva blessed Chandra, allowing him to regain his full form on the days following his decay. Daksha's curse caused him to decay again when he regained his power, but thanks to Shiva's blessings, the curse could not completely destroy Chandra. The

Shivalinga established and worshipped by Chandra became known as Somnath (the savior of the moon). Those suffering from physical ailments visit the Somnath temple for blessings.

The Somnath Temple is one of the twelve Jyotirlinga temples.

25

MAHAKALESHWAR

There was once a famous ancient city called Avanti, known for its beauty and rich culture. In this city lived a scholarly Brahmin named Vedapriya. He was deeply committed to spiritual practices and had mastered the holy texts. Vedapriya was admired throughout Avanti for his charitable nature and piety.

As a devout follower of Lord Shiva, Vedapriya performed Shiva Pujas in his own home. He had established a Shivaling there, and his dedicated worship made him well-respected among the people of Avanti. Vedapriya was blessed with four sons,

Devapriya, Priyamedha, Sukritan, and Suvratan, all of whom were also devoted to Shiva. Their righteous deeds brought joy and peace to the entire city.

However, a ruthless Asura named Bhooshana, who resided on Mount Ratnamala, posed a great threat. After years of meditation, Bhooshana was granted a boon by BrahmaDev. Empowered by his new strength, the Asura began attacking the Devas and Rishis, conquering the Vedas and sciences. With an army of minions, he stormed into Avanti, wreaking havoc, attacking sages and Brahmins, and destroying centres of knowledge and worship.

The citizens of Avanti fled in terror, but the four sons of Vedapriya remained steadfast. While the other Brahmins panicked, the four sons reassured them, saying, "O learned Brahmins, have faith in Lord Shiva. He will protect us."

Undeterred by the Asura's attacks, the four brothers continued their Shiva Puja. Hearing of their defiance, Bhooshana arrived and ordered, "Seize these Brahmins and kill them!"

The four Brahmin boys ignored his threats and continued their prayers. Furious, Bhooshana raised his weapon to strike them. Suddenly, a cavern appeared in the Shivaling, glowing with a brilliant light and accompanied by a deafening sound. To Bhooshana's shock, Lord Shiva emerged from the cavern, declaring, "I am Mahakala, an avatar of Shiva. My duty is to protect the innocent and destroy the wicked."

The Asura, taken aback, stepped back in fear. Mahakala continued, "Wicked one, I exist to slay malevolent beings like you. If you wish to be spared, apologize and flee, or I will annihilate you and your army."

But Bhooshana, filled with arrogance, laughed maniacally. With a single breath, Mahakala reduced Bhooshana and his entire army to ashes. The city of Avanti was liberated, and the citizens rejoiced, praising Lord Shiva for their deliverance.

Lord Shiva then turned to the four devotees and asked, "O scholarly Brahmins, ask for any boon, and I shall grant it."

The young Brahmins bowed before him and replied, "Dear Lord Mahakala, saviour of mankind, you have freed us from the demon. For the sake of future generations, we humbly request that you stay here so that we may continue to worship you."

Mahakala blessed them and agreed to remain present in the Shivaling, so that future generations could worship him. It is said that those who worship Mahakala are freed from sorrow.

Mahakaleshwar Temple in Ujjain is one of the twelve Jyotirlinga temples, where Lord Mahakala is revered to this day.

26

KEDARNATH

Nara and Narayana were twin brothers and incarnations of Lord Vishnu. Despite being avatars of Vishnu, they were devoted worshippers of Lord Shiva. The brothers created a Shivaling on a mountain in the Himalayas and began worshipping Shiva with great dedication.

Years passed as Nara and Narayana continued their worship without interruption, until one day, Lord Shiva appeared before them and said, "Dear devotees, I am pleased by your unwavering devotion. You have earned my blessings. Ask for any boon, and I shall grant it."

Nara and Narayana humbly replied, "O Lord Almighty, if you are truly pleased with our devotion, we ask that you stay here in your own form, so that others may also worship you. This is our only request."

Lord Shiva smiled and said, "So be it, my dear devotees."

He manifested as a Jyotirlinga and established himself on top of Mount Kedar in the Himalayas. From that moment, he became known as Kedarnath.

Many years later, after the Battle of Kurukshetra, the Pandavas sought to cleanse themselves of the sins they had incurred from the mass killings during the war. They knew of the Kedarnath Jyotirlinga in the Himalayas and set out on a pilgrimage through the rugged mountain paths to seek Lord Shiva's blessings.

However, Lord Shiva, knowing the Pandavas were coming, playfully avoided them. He fled to another part of the Himalayas and hid in a place called Gupta Kashi (Hidden Kashi), disguising himself as a Brahmin. But the Pandavas, determined to find him, soon uncovered his disguise. Realizing he had been found, Shiva fled again, this time taking the form of a bull and retreating to Mount Kedar.

Bhima, the strongest of the Pandavas, recognized the bull as Lord Shiva. With all his might, Bhima grabbed the bull by its tail. Shiva, still trying to conceal himself, began to bury himself into the ground. But the Pandavas' perseverance won him over.

Acknowledging the sincerity of their quest, Lord Shiva finally revealed himself to the Pandavas and blessed them. Moved by the encounter, the Pandavas built a sturdy temple around the Jyotirlinga for future generations to worship.

Though situated in one of the most remote and inhospitable regions of the world, Kedarnath Temple has become a revered site where devotees flock to catch a glimpse of Lord Shiva and seek his blessings.

Kedarnath Temple in the Himalayas is one of the twelve Jyotirlinga temples.

27

BHIMASHANKAR

In ancient times, deep within the jungle of the Sahyadri mountain range, there lived a cruel demon named Bhima, alongside his mother, Karkati. Compassion and kindness were nearly extinct in Bhima's presence, and the people lived in constant fear of him.

Curious about his origins, Bhima one day asked his mother to reveal the truth about his father. He asked, "Mother, tell me who my father was, and why he abandoned us in this wilderness. Please reveal the secret."

After much hesitation, and with a heavy heart, Karkati finally revealed the truth. "My son, it is time you learned the truth. You are the son of Kumbhakarna, the brother of Ravana, the King of Lanka."

Bhima exclaimed, "Kumbhakarna!? Where is he? What happened to him?"

Karkati replied, "Vishnu, in his incarnation as Rama, destroyed Kumbhakarna along with Ravana."

Shocked, Bhima shouted, "What!? Vishnu killed my father?"

Karkati continued, "That's not all, my son. You must hear the full story. My father was Karkata, and my mother was Pushkasi. My first husband was Viradhi, but he too was slain by Rama. After his death, I lived with my parents. One day, my parents attacked a sage named Sutishna, but the enraged Rishi cursed them to ashes. I was left alone. I wandered in grief until one day, Kumbhakarna visited the jungle. Obsessed with me, he wanted me as his wife, but I refused. However, he overpowered me and left me pregnant. He returned to Lanka, where he was eventually killed by Rama. I gave birth to you here, and I raised you alone. Now, you have grown strong and as malicious as your father."

Enraged by his mother's story, Bhima vowed, "I will avenge my father's death. Vishnu must pay for what he has done. It is because of him that my mother has suffered all her life. I will destroy him."

Determined to gain immense power, Bhima embarked on a severe penance to please Brahma. Impressed by Bhima's devotion, Brahma appeared before him and said, "Bhimasura, I am pleased with your dedication. Ask for any boon, and it shall be granted."

Bhimasura replied, "Grant me the power to be the strongest being in the world."

Brahma granted the wish and departed. However, this proved to be a grave mistake. Bhima immediately became more powerful and enormous. He rushed to his mother and boasted, "Mother, I am now invincible. I will destroy the Devas and Vishnu. You shall live in joy from now on."

With his newfound power, Bhima wreaked havoc across all three worlds. He defeated Indra and conquered Devaloka. Even Lord Vishnu, who came to aid Indra, was defeated by Bhima. The demon began torturing the Rishis and conquered all the Vedas and sciences. He stripped mortals of their resources and prevented them from worshipping the gods. The entire universe trembled under his tyranny.

In desperation, the Devas and Rishis went to Lord Shiva and pleaded, "O Almighty Lord, we know you are aware of the devastation Bhima is causing. He torments every living being. Please save us from this dreadful Asura."

Shiva, with calm assurance, replied, "I am aware, and I also know that Bhima has imprisoned my devoted follower, King Sudakshina. I will intervene soon."

Meanwhile, Sudakshina, bound in chains, continued his unwavering devotion to Lord Shiva by worshipping a Shivaling he created inside his prison cell. This infuriated Bhima, who demanded, "Worship me, not Shiva! Why do you waste your prayers on him? He has no power!"

Sudakshina boldly replied, "No, Lord Shiva is the mightiest of all. He could destroy you in an instant."

Angered, Bhima raised his sword to strike the Shivaling. But before he could act, Lord Shiva appeared in all his splendour, accompanied by a blinding light and a deafening sound.

Shiva declared, "Wicked demon, did you think I would not come? It is my duty to protect my devotees and to destroy evil beings like you."

A fierce battle ensued between Shiva and Bhima. Shiva effortlessly broke Bhima's sword in two and turned his trident into crumbling crystals. The fight raged on, shaking the balance of the world. At that moment, the sage Narada appeared and pleaded with Lord Shiva, "Almighty Lord, forgive me if I speak out of turn, but there is no need to use an axe to cut a blade of grass. The earth is on the verge of collapse. Please end Bhima's tyranny now."

Heeding Narada's words, Shiva turned Bhima to ashes, ending his reign of terror. The Devas and Rishis rejoiced and requested, "O Lord, please make this place your eternal abode so that all of humanity can worship you here."

Honoring their request, Lord Shiva manifested himself as the Bhimashankar Jyotirlinga.

The Bhimashankar Temple, located in the Sahyadri mountain range, is one of the twelve sacred Jyotirlinga temples.

28

VISHVESHWARA

At the beginning of the universe, Shiva became the embodiment of ParaBrahma, the supreme reality. Shiva encompassed both male and female forms, with the female part known as Shakti. Together, Shiva and Shakti created life (the Organism) and Nature.

Curious about their existence, Organism and Nature were unaware of their purpose and longed to know their creators. Suddenly, they received an inner call: "Both of you must meditate, and then you will be able to proliferate."

They replied, "Lord, we have no place to meditate."

In response, a magnificent and divine city appeared, radiating beauty and splendour. This entire city became theirs. The Organism, who was none other than Lord Vishnu, began to meditate there for the purpose of creation. Ages upon ages passed as Vishnu continued his deep meditation. He meditated with such intensity that he became exhausted, and from his exertion, he began to sweat. Over time, his sweat flooded the entire sky, forming a vast cosmic ocean. Weary from his meditation, Lord Vishnu lay upon the waters to rest.

As Vishnu slept on the waters, a gigantic lotus with mystical petals sprouted from his navel. This lotus was as radiant as the sun, and its beauty was indescribable. From the centre of this lotus, BrahmaDev emerged. Following the guidance of Lord Shiva, BrahmaDev took up his divine duty of creation.

BrahmaDev created fourteen worlds across the universe, covering an area of 500 million Yojanas. At that moment, Lord Shiva reflected, "Soon, these worlds will be populated with beings, but how will they reach out to me? Let the relic that Vishnu worshipped in this divine city become the sacred place for future generations to communicate with me."

Using his Trishula, Lord Shiva lifted the city and placed it on Earth. That city became known as Kashi.

When one day of BrahmaDev's life comes to an end, a great flood will destroy the world. Yet, Kashi will endure, surviving the deluge. During the flood, Lord Shiva will protect Kashi by holding it with his Trishula, and once BrahmaDev resumes his duty of creation, Shiva will once again place the city on Earth. In Kashi, anyone can attain Moksha (liberation).

Even the Devas aspire to have their deaths in Kashi, as Lord Shiva's presence there is palpable. In Kashi, Shiva is known as Vishveshwara or Vishwanath, the Lord of the Universe, and his divine presence can be felt by all who visit.

The Kashi Vishwanath Temple is the oldest of the twelve Jyotirlinga temples. Furthermore, the city of Kashi, also known as Varanasi, is recognized by historians as one of the oldest continuously inhabited city in the world.

29

TRIAMBAKESHWARA

Once upon a time in ancient India, there lived a sage named Gautama, who had a wife called Ahalya. As a result of his severe penance, Gautama was blessed with divine powers. One day, a terrible famine struck his kingdom, and the people began to starve. There wasn't even a leaf in sight due to the prolonged drought. With no hope of survival, all the beings, humans, animals, and birds, migrated elsewhere in search of sustenance.

Deeply concerned about the plight of his land, Gautama prayed to Varuna, the God of water. After six months of continuous penance, Varuna appeared before him and said, "Maharshi Gautama, I am pleased by your devotion. You may ask for any boon you desire."

Gautama humbly replied, "VarunaDev, the people of this kingdom are dying from starvation. We haven't been blessed with rain in years, and those who survived have fled. I request that you bring rain to this land and allow it to flourish with greenery once again."

Varuna smiled and said, "Maharshi, I will bless you with a permanent source of water, but you must first dig a pit."

Following Varuna's instructions, Gautama dug a small pit, only one foot deep. Varuna then filled the pit with divine water.

"This water will never dry up," Varuna said. "Consider this source sacred, and it shall be known by your name on Earth."

Maharshi Gautama generously shared the water with others, adhering to the rituals prescribed by Varuna to maintain its divine purity. He planted rice and other seeds in the fertile land around the well, and soon the fields yielded an abundance of crops and fruits. Word of this miraculous transformation spread, and people returned to the kingdom. Rishis, animals, and birds also came back and made the area their home. The once-barren land became lush and green, and the crops grown there nourished many Rishis and common people. With the blessings of the Rishis, Gautama's merit and fame grew even further.

However, Indra, the king of the gods, became envious of Gautama's rising popularity. He ordered the clouds to rain over the neighbouring areas, ensuring that there was no longer a shortage of food. His hope was that people would abandon Gautama and return to their lands. Despite this, Gautama urged the Rishis to stay, continuing to provide them with food and shelter. Many Brahmins and Maharshis remained at his ashram, performing their rituals in peace.

One day, Ahalya and some Brahmin women quarrelled over access to the water. Angered, the Brahmin women pressured their husbands to curse Gautama. Bowing to their wives' wishes, the Brahmins prayed to Lord Ganesh for a solution. Ganesh appeared before them and asked what they sought.

The Brahmins responded, "Lord Ganesh, we ask that all the followers in Gautama's ashram fall into discord. Let there be no harmony in his presence and let him be cast out of his own ashram."

Ganesh, displeased, replied, "Sages, what you ask is unjust. You are acting under the baseless urgings of your wives. Do not forget that it was Maharshi Gautama who saved you all from starvation during the famine. Now, you seek to harm him in return. Gautama is innocent, and your request will only bring you misery. I urge you to reconsider and ask for something else."

But the Brahmins, ignoring Ganesh's advice, insisted on their original wish.

Seeing their arrogance, Ganesh warned, "Since you refuse to heed my counsel, I will grant your wish, but know that it will lead to your downfall."

With that, Lord Ganesh disappeared.

Ganesha transformed into a stray cow and entered Gautama's paddy field. When Gautama saw the cow grazing, he tried to drive it away by throwing a handful of *Darbha* (sharp, pointed grass). Unfortunately, the cow died from the impact of the grass.

The Brahmins and their wives, who had been watching, immediately blamed Gautama for the tragic incident. Shocked and distressed, Gautama panicked and didn't know how to respond. Ahalya approached him, noticing his distress, and asked what was troubling him.

Gautama said, "Ahalya, I have no idea how this happened. Maybe Lord Shiva is testing me, or perhaps he's angry at me for some reason. I don't know what to do. What should I do?"

The Brahmins and their wives seized the opportunity to publicly shame him, criticizing him for the unfortunate event. When Ahalya tried to defend her husband, they even harmed her. Gautama, deeply ashamed, bowed his head in sorrow, but the Brahmins were still not satisfied.

They said, "Gautama, you must leave this ashram immediately. As long as you stay here, the Devas and the gods will not favour us. They will withhold their blessings. You have become a sinner by committing *Gowhatya* (the sin of killing a cow). Leave this place at once!"

The Brahmins and their wives began throwing stones at Gautama and Ahalya. With tearful eyes, Gautama pleaded, "Please, Brahmins, do not harm us. We will leave right away."

Obeying the Brahmins' command, Gautama left the ashram and established a new one nearby. When the Brahmins learned that Gautama had set up a new ashram and was about to perform Yajnas and Pujas, they hurried to confront him.

They declared, "Gautama, you are a sinner. As long as the stain of your crime remains, you must not perform any Yajna."

Gautama replied, "But how can I live without worshipping God? I will do anything to atone for my sins."

With contempt, the Brahmins shouted, "You must bring the sacred river Ganga here and bathe in its waters to cleanse yourself. And you must create ten million *Shivalingas* and worship them."

Determined to atone, Gautama, with the help of Ahalya, made ten million Shivalingas and began their worship. After years of continuous devotion, Lord Shiva appeared before him.

Shiva asked, "Dear Maharshi, I am pleased with your devotion. What wish would you like me to grant?"

Gautama bowed before Lord Shiva and said, "Oh Lord Almighty, please wash away my sins."

Shiva replied, "Maharshi, you are innocent. You have committed no sin. Who has declared you a sinner? They have deceived you. They are the real sinners. You, Maharshi, are so divine that you possess the power to absolve the sins of others."

Gautama was shocked by this revelation. He had not expected such a response from Lord Shiva.

He said, "Dear Lord, in a way, the Brahmins were instruments of fate. Without their actions, I would never have had the fortune of seeing you in person. Therefore, I do not hold them guilty. I am blessed because of what happened."

Shiva was deeply pleased by Gautama's humility.

He said, "Gautama, you are truly mystical. You are the greatest among living Rishis. I am very pleased with you. Ask for another wish, and I will grant it."

Gautama responded, "Oh Lord, I have but one wish. For the sake of the innocent souls here, I request you to bring the holy river Ganga to this place."

Gautama touched Lord Shiva's feet in reverence, and Shiva blessed him. Lord Shiva commanded the celestial river Ganga to flow near Gautama's ashram. Ganga agreed and began flowing through the region. Because of her association with Gautama's ashram, the river came to be known as Godavari. To further bless the devotees, Lord Shiva established a Jyotirlinga in the ashram, which eventually became a temple. This Jyotirlinga became known as *Triambaka.*

The Triambakeshwara Temple by the banks of the Godavari River is one of the twelve Jyotirlinga Temples.

30

VAIDYANATH

Ravana, the King of Lanka, was a fierce tyrant and an arrogant Asura, but he was also a devout follower of Lord Shiva. One day, he decided to pray to Lord Shiva at Mount Kailash. However, when Shiva did not grant him an audience, Ravana undertook a severe penance. He chose the southern region of the Himalayas for his meditation, established a Shivalinga there, and began performing a Yajna.

Ravana continued his worship through harsh winters and torrential monsoons, yet Lord Shiva still did not appear. Undeterred, Ravana took an extreme step to please Shiva:

he began cutting off his heads as offerings. One by one, he decapitated himself, sacrificing nine of his ten heads.

Just as Ravana was about to cut off his tenth and final head, Lord Shiva appeared before him, impressed by his devotion. Shiva restored Ravana's nine heads and granted him the powers he desired.

Overjoyed, Ravana said, "O Lord of All, I wish to take you back with me to Lanka. Please grant me this wish."

After thinking for a moment, Lord Shiva replied, "Asura King, I will grant your wish. I will give you a Jyotirlinga that you can take to Lanka and worship. However, there is one condition: if you ever place it on the ground, it will remain fixed there permanently and cannot be moved."

With that, Lord Shiva handed Ravana the Shivalinga.

Alarmed by this development, the Devas and Rishis objected. They knew that if Lord Shiva were to go to Lanka with Ravana, he would become invincible, and his evil deeds would threaten the world. They couldn't bear to see Shiva aiding Ravana.

To stop Ravana, the Devas devised a plan. They asked Varuna, the god of water, to enter Ravana's body on his journey back to Lanka. Soon after, Ravana felt a strong urge to relieve himself. But he knew that if he put the Shivalinga down, it would be stuck forever.

Ravana thought, "I need to find someone to hold the Shivalinga while I relieve myself."

As fate would have it, Lord Vishnu appeared in the guise of a Brahmin. Ravana, unaware of the trick, handed the Shivalinga to the Brahmin. However, Ravana could not return quickly enough, and in the meantime, the Brahmin placed the Shivalinga on the ground. As Shiva had warned, the Shivalinga immediately became immovable.

Ravana tried with all his strength to lift it, but it wouldn't budge.

Disheartened, he returned to Lanka empty-handed. The Devas rejoiced, knowing the Shivalinga was no longer in Ravana's possession.

Though Ravana still possessed great power due to Shiva's blessings, the Devas were not satisfied. They feared his strength and sought to diminish it further. They asked Narada, the celestial sage known for his cunning, to intervene.

Narada visited Ravana and said, "Oh mighty King of Lanka, Ravana the Great! I hear you possess divine powers granted by Lord Shiva himself."

Ravana proudly replied, "Yes, I am indeed blessed."

Narada, frowning, said, "Are you sure? Have you tested this power?"

Ravana, confused, asked, "What do you mean? I have the power. There is no doubt."

Narada leaned closer and said, "You should test your power before relying on it in battle."

After pondering this, Ravana said, "You're right, Narada. How should I test my strength?"

Narada suggested, "It's simple. Try to lift Mount Kailash. It is the heaviest mountain in existence. If you can lift it, you can truly accomplish anything."

Falling into Narada's trap, Ravana attempted to lift Mount Kailash, unaware that Lord Shiva and Parvati were seated upon it. The mountain began to tremble, disturbing Shiva. When Shiva realized that it was his devotee Ravana causing the commotion, he cursed him in anger.

"Ravana!" Shiva roared. "I blessed you with power, and now you use it to harm me? How dare you behave so arrogantly! You will pay for this. Your pride in your invincibility will be your downfall. A human will be born to destroy you. Beware!"

The Devas rejoiced at the success of their plan. True to Shiva's curse, Lord Rama was born to defeat Ravana. As for the Shivalinga that Ravana lost, which was placed on the ground by Vishnu, it became known as the *Vaidyanath* form of Lord Shiva.

The Vaidyanath Temple is one of the twelve Jyotirlinga temples.

31

NAGESHWAR

There once lived an infamous demoness named Daruki. Arrogant and vile, Daruki had received her power through the blessings of Goddess Parvati. She was married to a ruthless Rakshasa named Daruka. Together, they terrorized the innocent, frequently teaming up with other Rakshasas to plunder and attack people. Daruka especially enjoyed disrupting Yajnas and other sacred rituals performed by humans.

Daruki had a lush forest near the western sea, gifted to her by Parvati. This prosperous forest was abundant in resources, but Daruka and Daruki used it as a base for their cruel activities, torturing the people who lived there. The suffering villagers prayed to Lord Shiva, pleading for his help.

Shiva appeared before them and asked, "I sense that something troubles you. Tell me, my dear devotees, what is the cause of your distress?"

The people replied, "O Lord, the Rakshasa couple Daruka and Daruki torment us. They abduct our children, disrupt our Yajnas, and will not let us live in peace. Please, we beg you to help us."

Upset by their plight, Lord Shiva declared, "Do not worry, my devotees. I curse Daruka, so that the moment he harms another living being on earth, he will die instantly."

The Devas heard of this curse and saw an opportunity to rid the world of Daruka. Confident that he wouldn't be able to retaliate without dying, they launched an attack on him.

Daruka, realizing that the Devas were coming to kill him, was filled with panic. His wife, Daruki, tried to calm him, saying, "Beloved, by the powers granted to me by Goddess Parvati, I can move this entire forest to any place I choose. Do not worry."

Just before the Devas invaded, Daruki used her powers to transport the entire forest, submerging it beneath the sea. The couple continued to live there, free from the threat of the Devas. However, the creatures of the ocean soon began to suffer at the hands of the demons.

One day, several fishing boats unknowingly ventured into the waters near the demons' submerged forest. Daruka and Daruki surfaced and captured every person on the boats, imprisoning them in an underwater dungeon. The demons threatened and tortured the captives. Among the prisoners was a devout Vaishya named Supriya, who was a faithful follower of Lord Shiva. Supriya refused to eat or drink without first performing his daily worship of Shiva. Even in the dungeon, he made a Shivalinga from the materials available and continued his prayers. His unwavering devotion inspired the other prisoners, and soon, they all began chanting "Om Namah Shivaya."

Daruka was furious when he discovered this. He sent one of his demons to kill Supriya. The demon stormed into the cell, grabbed Supriya, and snarled, "I will tear you apart!" But Supriya remained calm and prayed, "O Lord Shiva, you who protect the innocent and destroy evil, please rescue us from these malevolent beings. You are our only hope."

Suddenly, Lord Shiva appeared in all his glory. Miraculously, a shrine with four doors materialized around the Shivalinga that Supriya had created. The Shivalinga began to glow with divine light. The prisoners rushed to the shrine, worshipping the Shivalinga and offering prayers to Lord Shiva. The demon was stunned, unable to comprehend what had just happened.

Shiva, wielding his weapon, annihilated Daruka and all the other demons in the underwater forest. He then raised the submerged forest back to the mainland. Once there, Shiva declared, "From this day forward, this forest will be a sanctuary for Brahmins, Kshatriyas, Vaishyas, and Shudras. No demon shall ever disturb their Dharmic duties again. This place will become a haven for scholars and sages, free from the torment of Rakshasas."

Daruki, having survived the massacre, prayed to Goddess Parvati. When Parvati appeared, she asked, "What is it that you desire, my devotee?"

Daruki pleaded, "O Goddess, please save my people. After Lord Shiva's wrath, our clan is on the verge of extinction. I promise that we will no longer harm anyone."

Parvati, moved by her plea, approached Lord Shiva and said, "Beloved, please spare the remaining Rakshasas. Let them live in peace, as long as they do not harm others. Allow Daruki to lead her people and guide them toward a righteous life."

Shiva replied, "Devi, I cannot refuse you. However, I have made this land a sanctuary for innocent beings, and I must protect them. If these Rakshasas cause harm again, my divine presence will remain here for the people to worship. They will live without fear of any evil forces."

Thus, the Jyotirlinga at that site became the Nageshwar form of Lord Shiva, and the temple that arose there became known as the Nageshwara Temple.

Nageshwara Temple is one of the twelve Jyotirlinga Temples.

32

RAMESHWAR

Lord Vishnu incarnated as Sri Rama during the Treta Yuga with a singular purpose: to destroy the Adharmic Asura, Ravana, the king of Lanka. Sri Rama's fate led him to live an exiled life in the jungle alongside his wife, Sita, and his brother, Lakshmana. During this time, Ravana abducted Sita, prompting Rama to embark on a mission to rescue her from Ravana's grasp and liberate the people of Lanka from the demon king's tyranny. With the help of his brother Lakshmana and Hanuman, Rama set out for Lanka.

Rama and the Vanara army eventually reached the seashore

that separated India from Lanka. Standing before the vast ocean, Rama grew anxious.

"How can I cross this ocean? How can I defeat Ravana?" Rama wondered aloud.

Suddenly, he felt thirsty. The Vanaras brought him some sweet water, and as he drank, Rama had a vision of Lord Shiva.

Hanuman noticed Rama's contentment and asked, "You seem happy. Have you found a solution to our problem?"

Rama smiled and replied, "Yes! I must pray to Lord Shiva. He is the symbol of hope for all that is good."

Setting down the bowl of water, Rama fashioned a Shivalinga on the ground and began to perform puja. His sincere devotion pleased Lord Shiva, who appeared before him.

Filled with reverence, Sri Rama said, "O Great Lord of All! You are my Master, and I am your humble servant. I can only succeed with your blessings. Ravana, though ruthless, is your devoted follower. It is your boon that has made him invincible, and his arrogance and ego have driven him to seek dominance over the three worlds. He must be stopped to restore balance to the universe. But I cannot accomplish this task without your divine grace, my Lord."

Bowing low, Rama repeatedly chanted, "Jai Shankara! Jai Shiva!"

Lord Shiva, pleased by Rama's devotion, said, "Rama, you will be successful. I am content with your devotion."

Rama, with gratitude, asked, "O Lord, Sada Shiva, please grant me the strength to defeat Ravana in the battle at Lanka."

"So be it. You will emerge victorious, as you wish," Lord Shiva blessed him.

Rama then made a request, "Lord, if you are truly satisfied with my devotion, please remain here so that all can worship you at this sacred spot."

In response to Rama's request, the Shivalinga that he had established became a Jyotirlinga, known as Rameshwara. It remains a revered site of worship to this day. The Rameswara Temple in Tamil Nadu is one of the Twelve Jyotirlinga Temples.

33

GHUSHMESHWAR

Devagiri was a mountain in the Deccan region of India, renowned for its scenic beauty. There lived a pious Brahmin named Sudharma and his wife, Sudeha. The couple was deeply engaged in spiritual practices. Sudharma lived a life of Dharma, giving generously to the poor and organizing Yagas. He strictly followed the Vedas and lived by its teachings. As a devoted follower of Lord Shiva, Sudharma also taught his disciples the righteous ways of life, raising many scholars who became assets to the kingdom.

However, despite their devoutness, Sudharma and Sudeha

were not blessed with a child. While Sudharma accepted this fate without complaint, Sudeha was deeply distressed by their childlessness. She yearned for a child and could not find solace in her husband's comforting words.

One day, Sudeha brought her sister, Ghushma, to Sudharma and said, "My dear husband, I request you to marry Ghushma so that we may have a child through her."

Sudharma replied, "I have no objection to your wish, but I am concerned about you. It is possible that you may grow resentful of your sister after we have a child."

Sudeha assured him, "No, I will not. I will consider her child as mine. I will never harbour hatred toward my sister."

With this reassurance, Sudharma married Ghushma. After the marriage, Ghushma served her sister with utmost devotion. Following Sudharma's guidance, Ghushma made 101 Shivalingas every day and immersed them in a pond after performing Shiva Puja. Pleased with her devotion, Lord Shiva blessed Ghushma, and soon, she became pregnant and gave birth to a son. Sudharma and Ghushma were overjoyed, but Sudeha grew increasingly jealous.

Years passed, and the boy grew into a handsome young man. He married a beautiful woman, and they lived happily with his parents. However, Sudeha's envy festered, and she sought to destroy the happiness of the family. Consumed by jealousy, she devised a plan to murder her nephew.

One night, while the young man slept alone in his room, Sudeha crept in with a sword and brutally killed him, hacking his body into pieces. In her madness, she gathered the dismembered body and threw the pieces into the same pond where Ghushma had been immersing the Shivalingas.

The next morning, Ghushma performed her daily puja as usual. When she returned home, her daughter-in-law was searching frantically for her husband. Together, they searched the house and eventually found bloodstains in the young man's room.

Ghushma cried out in anguish, while her daughter-in-law collapsed in despair. "Dear mother, can't you see? Your son has been brutally murdered! You have devoted yourself to God, yet fate has been cruel to us. Who could have committed such an atrocity?"

Sudeha, pretending to be shocked, feigned concern and said, "Oh my God! I can't believe this! Who would kill such a good young man?"

Despite their grief, Ghushma and Sudharma remained composed and continued their worship of Lord Shiva. The following day, Ghushma returned to the pond to immerse her Shivalingas. To her astonishment, she saw her son standing by the water, alive and unharmed. She realized that this was the blessing of Lord Shiva. Suddenly, Lord Shiva appeared before her and said, "Ghushma, I am pleased with your devotion. It was your sister, Sudeha, who tried to murder your son. But do not worry, I have restored him to life in full glory. Sudeha deserves to die by the tips of my Trishula. Now, ask for any wish you desire."

Ghushma bowed before Shiva and said, "O Lord Shiva, the God of All, Sudeha is my elder sister. I ask you to forgive her."

Shiva replied, "Your sister has committed a grave sin. Why do you seek mercy for her?"

Ghushma responded, "My Lord, seeing your divine presence has erased all my grief. I wish for my sister's sins to be turned to ashes, and for her to be guiltless."

Deeply moved by Ghushma's compassion, Lord Shiva said, "Ghushma, I will grant your request and absolve your sister's sins. But as my favorite devotee, you may ask for any other boon as well."

Ghushma replied, "O Lord, if you are truly pleased with me, I ask that you remain here at this sacred place so that everyone may worship you. I would be honored if you would be known by my name here."

Shiva smiled and said, "I will be known as Ghushmeshwar at this holy site. Anyone who worships me here will be blessed. Your descendants will be successful and become great scholars."

Thus, a Jyotirlinga was formed at that spot, and it became known as Ghushmeshwar or Grishneshwar. The Grishneshwar Temple is revered as one of the twelve Jyotirlinga temples.

34

MALLIKARJUNA

The story of how Mount Krounch became the sacred site known as Mallikarjuna is connected to Kartikeya's return from his travels around the world. However, there is another legend behind this same Jyotirlinga temple.

Once, there was a princess named Chandravathi in a southern kingdom. She was incredibly beautiful, and her beauty attracted many admirers. Unfortunately, she also faced unwanted advances from members of her own royal family. Being a devout and pious woman, Chandravathi wished to renounce all material attachments and live a life of purity and devotion.

Determined to lead a sanctified life, Chandravathi abandoned her royal lifestyle and left for the forest of Srisailam. She gave away her jewelry and other possessions to the poor and began living as a hermit, relying on the forest for sustenance. As the days passed, she survived on the fruits of the forest but grew increasingly hungry.

One day, she spotted a wild cow roaming through the forest and thought, "I could drink milk from one of these cows." Chandravathi approached the cow, but it suddenly ran away, leaving her without any milk that day.

The next day, she saw the same cow again. This time, instead of approaching it, she observed the cow from a distance. The cow seemed to be heading toward a specific location with purpose. Intrigued, Chandravathi decided to follow the cow and see where it was going.

The following day, she waited at the same spot and, as expected, saw the cow once again. Quietly, she followed it without disturbing its path. The cow eventually stopped at a secluded area. Hidden behind a tree, Chandravathi watched as the cow walked up to a small Shivalinga that was covered in jasmine creepers. Standing over the Shivalinga, the cow poured its milk onto the sacred object. Chandravathi was astonished at what she witnessed. It was nothing short of a miracle.

That night, while she was asleep, Chandravathi had a divine vision. Lord Shiva appeared before her and said, "Dear Chandravathi, establish a temple over the divine Shivalinga you saw today."

When she awoke, Chandravathi wondered whether the previous night's events had been a dream or reality. But then she realized, "This is a divine instruction from Lord Shiva."

Following Lord Shiva's command, Chandravathi gathered the people of the region and built a temple at the spot where the jasmine-covered Shivalinga stood. As the temple was being constructed, the Shivalinga began to radiate with a brilliant, divine light. The people exclaimed with joy, "This is a Jyotirlinga!" They thanked Chandravathi for founding the temple and honored her as a spiritual leader.

Because the Shivalinga was covered with "mallige" (jasmine), the temple became known as Mallikarjuna. Over time, the Mallikarjuna Temple was revered as one of the twelve Jyotirlinga temples.

35

OMKARESHWAR

Sage Narada was returning to Devalok after worshipping Lord Shiva on Earth. On his way, he came across the mighty Vindhya mountain range. Seeing the revered sage, Vindhya prepared a warm and hospitable atmosphere for Narada's stay. Filled with pride, Vindhya said, "Oh Sage Narada, I'm sure you've never seen a place as beautiful as this. I possess all the resources in the world - abundant water, trees full of fruit, and rich plant life. The Rishis, animals, and everyone living here depend on my generosity. Surely, you've never encountered another mountain as rich and revered as I am. I am the tallest and the strongest."

Narada was irritated by Vindhya's boastfulness. With calmness, he replied, "Mighty Vindhya, I must say, you've been a wonderful host. I couldn't receive such warm treatment anywhere else. However, there is something that disturbs me."

Vindhya was taken aback. "Oh no! I have everything here. There is no lack of resources. But why are you unhappy? Do you think something is missing?"

Narada replied, "Vindhya, I know you have everything. But compared to the great Mount Meru, you are still small. Meru is so tall that its summit reaches Devalok itself."

After saying this, Narada left. Vindhya felt deeply saddened by Narada's words.

He thought, "All my life, I believed I was the mightiest of mountains. My entire existence revolves around this belief. But now, it seems I am insignificant. I need to find purpose to continue. There is only one God who can give me an answer."

Vindhya decided to worship Lord Shiva. He made a Shivaling and began his worship, undertaking severe penance for six months. Pleased by Vindhya's unwavering devotion, Lord Shiva appeared before him and said, "Dear Vindhya, I did not know you were such a dedicated devotee of mine. I am extremely pleased by your worship. You may ask for any boon, and I shall grant it."

Vindhya replied, "Oh Almighty God! I ask for the ability to perform all tasks efficiently and with expertise."

Shiva said, "So be it! Your decision to become a valuable asset for all mankind is wise and worthy."

Knowing that Lord Shiva had blessed Vindhya, the Rishis and scholars residing in the area prayed, "Oh Lord Shiva, please remain here so that we may continue to worship you."

Thus, the Shivaling Vindhya had created turned into a Jyotirlinga, which came to be known as Omkareshwar.

Omkareshwar Temple is recognized as one of the twelve Jyotirlinga temples.

36

VISHNU WORSHIPS SHIVA

During one of the many periods of Asura domination, the Asuras conquered the three worlds after defeating the Devas. Most of the Devas were imprisoned in the dungeons of Patala, while the Asuras' reign of Adharma tormented countless innocent beings. A few surviving Devas, still free, approached Lord Vishnu for help.

"We need your assistance," they begged. "The Asuras are destroying the world with their tyrannical rule."

"Let me see what I can do," Vishnu replied and joined the battle.

However, even Lord Vishnu found himself overwhelmed by the power of the Asuras. Realizing that if he continued to fight, he would be completely annihilated, Vishnu retreated from the battlefield. The Devas were dismayed, but Vishnu reassured them. "Do not worry, fellow Devas. There is still hope."

The Devas, in despair, responded, "What do you mean? You are our ultimate protector. If you cannot defeat the Asuras, then we are surely doomed."

Vishnu smiled and said, "Perhaps you have forgotten about Lord Shiva. He is the Supreme God, the Almighty. With his support, we will surely be victorious. I will go to him and pray. He will come to our aid."

The Devas shouted with joy and renewed hope.

Lord Vishnu then journeyed to Mount Kailas, where he fashioned a Shivaling out of snow and began to worship it. He chanted the *Sahasranama* (a thousand names of Lord Shiva) while offering lotuses one by one. Meanwhile, Lord Shiva, wanting to test Vishnu's devotion, used his divine power (Maya) to hide one of the thousand lotuses that Vishnu had brought for the Puja.

Unaware of Shiva's trick, Vishnu continued his worship. When he reached the final offering, he discovered that he was missing the thousandth lotus. Disheartened, he searched the world for the missing flower but could not find it. Undeterred, Vishnu did not panic. In a supreme act of devotion, he decided to complete the ritual by plucking out one of his own lotus-like eyes and offering it to the Shivaling.

Pleased by this act of pure and selfless devotion, Lord Shiva appeared before Vishnu and said, "Dear Vishnu, I am deeply contented by your worship. You may have your eye back. Ask any boon, and I shall gladly grant it."

Vishnu replied, "Oh Lord Shiva, the Supreme God, the Almighty, I am your humble servant. You are omnipotent and omniscient. You know of the recent attacks by the Asuras. They are tormenting all beings in the three worlds, and the Devas are powerless against them. At present, I am not strong enough to defeat them. I humbly request you to grant me a powerful weapon."

Lord Shiva took one of his own weapons, the Sudarsana Chakra, and said, "I crafted this powerful disc during my battle against Jalandhara. It is the weapon I used to decapitate him. Now, I gift this to you."

Shiva thus bestowed the Sudarsana Chakra upon Vishnu. With this invincible weapon, Vishnu destroyed the Asuras, ending their dominance over the three worlds and restoring peace.

37

GURUGUHA THE HUNTER

Long ago, in a dense jungle, there lived a tribal hunter named Guruguha with his family. He was strong and fierce, often attacking travelers and stealing their belongings. He sustained his family by hunting animals but never engaged in any charitable or devotional activities.

One evening, on the day of Shivaratri, Guruguha's parents, hungry and restless, said, "Son, we are starving. Why are you sitting idle? Go deeper into the jungle and hunt some animals. We need something to eat immediately."

Unaware of the spiritual significance of Shivaratri, during which fasting and abstinence bring blessings, the hunter had no idea that the day held any importance. Coincidentally, he had no luck finding food that day.

As dusk approached, despite his search throughout the jungle, he couldn't find a single animal to kill. Determined not to return home empty-handed, he resolved to hunt down an animal, no matter how long it took. Wandering through the forest, feeling dejected, he eventually arrived at a lake.

He thought to himself, "Surely, an animal will come here to drink water. I'll shoot it and take it back home. I just need to wait quietly for the opportunity."

Guruguha scooped some water from the lake into a bowl he carried, then climbed a nearby Bael tree and positioned himself on a branch to wait. Exhausted and hungry, the hunter soon dozed off.

In the first Yama (unit of time of ancient India) of the night, a deer approached the lake to drink. The sound of the deer roused the hunter. Excited, he fumbled for his bow and arrow. In his haste, he accidentally knocked the bowl of water, spilling some drops below. Unbeknownst to him, there was a Shivaling beneath the tree. The falling water and Bael leaves inadvertently

landed on the Shivaling, thus performing a proper Shiva Puja for the first Yama of Shivaratri. As a result, some of the hunter's accumulated sins were burned away, and he gained a slight sense of enlightenment.

The deer, startled by the sound, looked up and saw the hunter aiming at her with his bow and arrow. In desperation, the deer spoke, "Oh noble hunter, please listen to my plea."

Guruguha was astonished, "A talking deer?" He lowered his bow and arrow, curious to hear what she had to say.

"Please don't kill me, hunter," the deer begged.

The hunter replied, "My family is starving back home. They haven't eaten anything all day. I need to kill you to feed them tonight."

The deer responded, "I would consider it a blessing if my flesh could feed your family. If my life can serve the purpose of sustaining others, then I will attain Moksha. I won't resist being your prey. But I have a request. Back home, my children are alone. They will be distressed if they can't find me. I beg you to let me return home first to entrust my children to my sister and her husband, who will care for them. I promise I will return after that, and you may do as you wish."

Guruguha hesitated. "How can I trust you? This could be a trick to escape."

The deer reassured him, "I swear by my promise. Breaking it would be a sin, and I would suffer the consequences. Please trust me."

Reluctantly, the hunter agreed. "Very well, you may go, but return quickly."

The deer galloped back home, and by then, the first Yama had ended.

Shortly afterward, the sister of the first deer arrived at the lake to drink water. Once again, the hunter raised his bow and arrow, but as he aimed, he accidentally knocked the bowl, causing more water and Bael leaves to fall onto the Shivaling below. Inadvertently, he performed Shiva Puja for the second Yama of Shivaratri, and his enlightenment deepened.

Seeing the hunter, the second deer cried out, "Hunter! What are you doing?"

"I need food for my starving family," the hunter replied. "I must kill you for that."

"If that's the case, then I am blessed," the deer said. "My flesh will serve a noble purpose. But before you kill me, I have a request."

"Speak quickly," the hunter replied.

"My children are alone at home, and I must inform my husband so he can care for them. I promise to return after that, and you may take my life."

"Why should I trust you?" the hunter asked. "I should kill you now."

The deer replied, "I've made a promise. Breaking it would be a sin worse than death. Please trust me."

Guruguha reluctantly agreed, and the deer ran home. By then, the second Yama had ended. The hunter grew worried that the first deer had not yet returned and kept a close watch on the lake.

Just then, a large buck came to the lake. Once again, the hunter awkwardly raised his bow and arrow. In his haste, he knocked over the bowl, spilling water and Bael leaves onto the Shivaling. Thus, he performed the Shiva Puja for the third Yama of Shivaratri, and his spiritual awareness increased even more.

The buck, hearing the commotion, looked up and saw the hunter. "Stay still!" the hunter shouted. "I will kill you to feed my family!"

The buck calmly replied, "If my flesh can nourish your family, I am blessed. But before you kill me, I ask that you let me go and inform my children's mother, so she can care for them. I promise I will return immediately after."

The hunter calmly said, "Deer, the others that came before you gave me similar excuses, but they all betrayed me. If you deceive me like they did, how will I feed my family?"

The deer replied, "Hunter, I do not lie. Lying is a sin. Moreover, today is Shivaratri, a sacred day. How can I lie on such an auspicious occasion? It would be an eternal crime. Please believe me. I will return to you."

Guruguha agreed, and the deer went back to its home.

Unfortunately, when the three deer met at their dwelling and discussed their promises, they realized the shocking truth: they all had to sacrifice their lives, leaving their children behind.

The elder doe said to her husband, "Beloved, our children can't survive without you. Therefore, I will go. I promised the hunter before you. You should stay with my sister and care for the fawns."

The sister doe interjected, "No, dear sister. You must stay and raise the children with your husband. I was the first to make the promise to the hunter. I shall go."

The buck said, "Neither of you should go. The fawns need their mothers. I will be the one to make the sacrifice."

The elder doe responded, "Darling, I cannot live without you. And I must honor the promise I made."

In the end, the three deer resolved to fulfill their promises. They entrusted their fawns to a neighbor and set off to face the hunter. The fawns, unwilling to part from their parents, followed them, saying they would rather pursue the ultimate path of their parents.

When Guruguha saw the three deer and their fawns approaching, he was excited and prepared his bow and arrows. As before, he accidentally knocked the bowl, causing water and Bael leaves to fall onto the Shivaling below. In doing so, he unknowingly performed the Shiva Puja for the fourth and final Yama of Shivaratri. As a result, all his sins were burned away, and he became an enlightened man.

The three deer spoke, "Hunter, we have returned as promised. You may kill us and use our flesh to feed your family. We will attain Moksha by fulfilling the needs of others."

But the hunter, now transformed by his newfound enlightenment, thought to himself, "These animals are righteous, despite being simple creatures. They are ready to sacrifice their lives for others. Look at me, I was given the superior form of a human, and I wasted my life on selfish pursuits. I must atone for my sins."

Lowering his weapon, the hunter said, "Noble creatures, you are free to go. Your lives are too valuable. You have kept your promise and honored it with virtue. I will not kill you."

Suddenly, Lord Shiva appeared in all his splendor. He gently placed his hand on the hunter's head and said, "Guruguha, I am pleased with your penance. Your act of kindness has made you an honorable man. Ask for any boon, and I shall grant it."

Guruguha replied, "I have gained everything I could ever desire just by glimpsing your divine form." He bowed and touched Lord Shiva's feet.

Shiva smiled and said, "Guruguha, you will build a great palace in Sringaverapura and lead a royal life. Your legacy will endure without hardship. The Devas and Rishis will seek your counsel. One day, Lord Sri Rama will come to meet you, and you will serve as his companion. In the end, you will attain Moksha."

With Lord Shiva's blessings, the deer and their fawns were freed from their animal forms, attaining liberation.

38

KRISHNA WORSHIPS SHIVA

Krishna, though a great warrior and king, did not have a son. Eager to find a solution, he visited the ashram of Maharshi Upamanyu. The sage was delighted to see Krishna and asked, "Oh Sri Krishna! What brings you here?"

Krishna replied, "Maharshi Upamanyu, I am in desperate need of a son to carry on my legacy."

Upamanyu nodded and said, "Indeed, a hero like you must have someone to continue your lineage. There is a way. You must worship Lord Shiva, the Almighty. He will surely bless you with a son."

Krishna exclaimed, "You are right! I must serve Lord Shiva and bow at his feet. There is no doubt that Lord Shiva is the Supreme God."

Following Upamanyu's advice, Krishna traveled to the Himalayas, where he crafted a Shivaling from snow. He dedicated himself to strict penance and daily worship, performing puja to the Shivaling without fail.

One day, Lord Shiva appeared before Krishna, accompanied by Parvati and their sons, Ganesh and Kartikeya. Upon seeing Shiva, Krishna ran to him, bowed down, and touched his feet in reverence. He said, "Oh God Almighty, Lord of all, Supreme God, I am your humble servant. I bow before you."

Shiva, pleased with Krishna's devotion, replied, "Dear Krishna, I am content with your devotion. Tell me what you wish, and I will grant it."

Krishna said, "God Almighty, I wish for a son."

Shiva smiled and said, "Your wish is granted, Krishna. A son will be born to you. He will be named Samba and will possess great strength and valor like you. He will follow your commands and carry on your legacy."

Blessed by Shiva, Krishna continued to sing praises of him. Parvati, delighted by Krishna's devotion, said, "Son of Vasudeva, dear Krishna, your devotion has brought me joy. You may ask for any boon you desire."

Krishna replied, "Devi Parvati, if you are truly pleased with me, I humbly ask for this: that I may never feel disdain for scholars, that I may always revere them, that my parents be proud of my actions, and that I have the means to feed thousands of sages and guests. Above all, let me live in happiness."

Parvati blessed him, saying, "So be it, Krishna. You shall have all the splendours you seek."

Krishna worships Shiva

With the blessings of Lord Shiva and Parvati, Krishna returned to Maharshi Upamanyu to share the good news. Upamanyu, overjoyed, said, "Krishna, know this truth - there is no God mightier than Lord Shiva. He blesses his devotees and destroys evil, maintaining the balance of the universe. You are fortunate to have been blessed by him. Go forth and tell the world of Lord Shiva's power. Praise him always."

Krishna, following Upamanyu's advice, returned to Dwarka. As foretold, he was blessed with a son, Samba, born to him through Jambavati.

39

TIME FLIES

In ancient India, there were two prominent kings named Dharmadhwaja and Kushadhwaja. They ruled their kingdoms with justice and liberty, but unfortunately, they lost all their prosperity due to a curse from Surya Dev. To regain their lost wealth and fortune, they began to worship Lakshmi Devi, the Goddess of Fortune. The cause of this curse from Surya Dev is explained below.

An ancestor of Dharmadhwaja and Kushadhwaja, Vrishadhwaja, was a devoted follower of Lord Shiva. One day, he began a deep penance to worship Shiva, enduring the changing seasons for many years. Finally, Lord Shiva appeared before him and said, "O Vrishadhwaja, I am pleased with your devotion. Tell me, what boon do you seek?"

Vrishadhwaja replied, "I am overjoyed just to witness your divine presence, Lord. I have but one request: that you grace my abode with your presence for some time, so that I may acquire prosperity and auspiciousness through your blessing."

Shiva, pleased by his devotion, agreed. "My dear devotee, I will grant your wish. You will have the honor of my presence in your home, and it will bring you prosperity."

Thus, a Shivaling was established in Vrishadhwaja's home, and with the presence of Lord Shiva, Vrishadhwaja became even more devoted to him. He spent most of his time worshipping Shiva and began neglecting other gods. This infuriated Surya Dev, the Sun God, who said, "How dare you ignore the other gods in your blind devotion to Shiva? I am the mighty Sun who illuminates the world, and yet you disregard me! For this, I curse you: your descendants will lose all their wealth and prosperity."

When Shiva heard about this curse, he was greatly angered by Surya Dev's arrogance. He declared, "Vrishadhwaja is my devoted follower. Cursing him is an insult to me. I will destroy you for this, Surya!"

With his weapons in hand, Shiva rushed to kill Surya. Fearing his imminent destruction, Surya panicked and sought refuge with his father, Maharshi Kashyap. "Father, help me! Lord Shiva is coming to kill me," Surya pleaded.

Kashyap, hearing of Surya's behavior, replied, "Son, you have acted arrogantly, and now you deserve to face Shiva's wrath. But if you are destroyed, it will bring chaos to the world."

Surya begged, "It was a mistake! Please think of the consequences if I am destroyed."

Kashyap, though powerless to stop Shiva, said, "We must seek help from BrahmaDev."

They went to BrahmaDev's abode, where Kashyap said, "Dear BrahmaDev, Lord Shiva is coming to kill my son, Surya. The world will suffer if the Sun is destroyed. Please, help us calm Shiva's anger."

BrahmaDev replied, "Kashyap, I cannot stop Shiva. His wrath is beyond my power. Our only hope is Lord Vishnu. Let us seek his help."

Surya, Kashyap, and BrahmaDev then approached Lord Vishnu. BrahmaDev said, "Dear Lord Vishnu, Shiva is fast approaching to destroy Surya. The balance of the world depends on his existence. Please, help us pacify Shiva's anger."

Vishnu asked Surya, "What caused this conflict between you and Shiva?"

Surya explained, "Vrishadhwaja, a devotee of Shiva, gained immense wealth and prosperity due to Shiva's presence. In my frustration, I cursed his descendants."

Vishnu laughed and said, "You are all behaving like ignorant beings. Don't you realize how differently time flows on Earth compared to the Deva world? By the time you came here, hundreds of years have passed on Earth. Vrishadhwaja lived a prosperous life and passed away long ago. Even his son, Rathadhwaja, has died of old age. His grandsons, Dharmadhwaja and Kushadhwaja, are now on the throne, worshipping Lakshmi Devi to regain their lost fortune. There is no need for this conflict anymore. I will pacify Shiva."

With Lord Vishnu's intervention, Shiva's anger was calmed, and Surya was spared. Meanwhile, Dharmadhwaja and Kushadhwaja regained their fortune with the blessings of Goddess Lakshmi.

40

TRUE DEVOTION

Long ago, during the Kali Yuga, there lived a hunter named Tinna. He spent his entire life in the forest, hunting and gathering, and never learned anything about the civilization of the outside world. He was unaware of the proper modes of worship or the morals of society, living the life of an innocent hunter.

However, upon hearing praises of Lord Shiva, Tinna became a staunch devotee. He would make Shivalings out of rocks and sand, worshipping them with whatever methods he knew, however awkward they might be. Frequently, Tinna offered the flesh of hunted animals to the Shivaling and engaged in penance.

Content with Tinna's devotion, Shiva passively blessed him. Finding this strange, Goddess Parvati asked, "Beloved, I don't understand why you continue to bless that primitive barbarian. He is unclean and uncivilized, and he doesn't worship you properly. Yet you still bless him. Please explain, dear."

Lord Shiva smiled and replied, "Dear Parvati, Tinna may be uncivilized and unaware of proper moral codes, but his devotion is sincere. That is why I grant him my blessings."

Parvati, still doubtful, said, "I am not convinced by his worship, though."

Shiva replied, "I will prove it to you. Wait and watch."

The next day, Tinna was traveling to the outskirts of the forest when he saw a crowded Shiva temple. Delighted, he rushed to the spot with the meat he had gathered. As he was about to enter the temple, a priest shouted, "Hey you! How dare you make this place dirty with the blood and flesh of hunted animals? You unclean barbarian! Your presence alone pollutes this sacred space. Stand back or I will call the guards to punish you!"

Deeply sorrowed, Tinna kept his distance from the temple and watched the devotees entering with reverence. He wished he could worship Shiva in this holy place. Suddenly, the earth began to shake, and the roof of the temple started to collapse. The devotees, including the priests inside, ran away in fear. But Tinna rushed inside and covered the Shivaling with his body to protect it from damage.

Mysteriously, Tinna noticed that one of the eyes of the Shivaling was oozing blood. Thinking that Shiva's eye had been injured, Tinna used his arrow to pluck out one of his own eyes and placed it over the bleeding eye of the Shivaling, stopping the flow of blood. However, he soon realized that the other eye of the Shivaling had also begun to bleed.

Contemplating his next move, Tinna considered that if he plucked out his other eye, he would become blind and unable to position it correctly over the second bleeding eye of the Shivaling. After a moment of thought, he placed his great toe on the Shivaling to mark the spot of the second eye and then plucked out his remaining eye.

Out of the blue, Lord Shiva appeared before Tinna and said, "Oh my dear Tinna, I am extremely pleased with your devotion. Here, I have restored your eye. Your faith in me is profound, and you worship without seeking returns. Please tell me what you wish for, and I will grant it to you."

Tinna replied, "Oh mighty Lord, my only wish is to worship you without any hindrance and to spread your bliss to others."

Shiva announced, "Tinna, from now on you will be known as Kannappa. You will become a great scholar and a teacher."

Thus, Tinna became Kannappa, one of the 63 Nayanmars, or saints, who spread the divine message of God.

41

MARKANDEYA

In ancient times, there lived a Maharshi named Mrikandu, a devout man and a strong devotee of Lord Shiva. He was well-known in the kingdom for his charitable nature and generous personality. However, despite all his virtues, he and his wife were not blessed with a child, which caused his wife deep sorrow. Mrikandu performed many Pujas and spiritual rituals, but all his efforts seemed in vain. Finally, he decided to undergo severe penance to please Lord Shiva.

After several years of meditation, Shiva appeared before him and said, "I sense sorrow within you. Tell me, dear devotee, what you wish for."

Markandeya

Mrikandu replied, "Dear Lord, my wife and I long for a son."

Shiva then asked, "Do you wish for a righteous and scholarly son who will live only sixteen years, or do you prefer a son who will live a long life but be cruel and vicious?"

Without hesitation, Mrikandu answered, "God of All, I desire a virtuous son."

Shiva blessed Mrikandu and disappeared. Mrikandu returned home and joyfully shared the good news with his wife.

In time, his wife became pregnant and gave birth to a boy, whom they named Markandeya. Like his parents, Markandeya grew into an honorable and pious child. He regularly visited the Shiva temple and performed Puja on his own. He became a scholar of the Vedas and sciences, earning the admiration of his teachers. Markandeya blossomed into a fully enlightened young scholar.

Yet, despite his brilliance, his parents were consumed by worry as he grew older. They were haunted by the knowledge that his life was destined to end at the age of sixteen. Though they prayed relentlessly, hoping to extend his life, they eventually accepted his fate. They couldn't hide their sorrow from Markandeya.

Sensing his parents' grief, Markandeya approached them one day and asked, "Mother, Father, I can feel that something is troubling you. Please tell me what's wrong."

With a heavy heart, Mrikandu replied, "There is no point in hiding the truth from you. You are a blessing from Lord Shiva, but your life is fated to be short. You are destined to die at the age of sixteen. We have tried everything to change this, but nothing has worked. It seems you must face the inevitable."

Markandeya's mother broke into tears. He comforted her and said, "Mother, don't cry. There is no need to worry. As long as Lord Shiva is by our side, nothing will happen to me. Death is inevitable for every being in the universe; the only difference is the age at which it comes and what awaits in the afterlife."

Determined, Markandeya went to the seashore and made a Shivaling out of sand, where he began worshipping Shiva with unwavering devotion. He never missed a single day of Puja.

Years passed, and Markandeya finally reached the age of sixteen. One day, while he was worshipping Shiva, he saw a chariot descending from the sky. Yama's minions had come to claim him.

A minion announced, "Markandeya, it is time for you to leave your earthly life. We have come to take you to Yamalok."

Markandeya replied, "Do not disturb my Shiva Puja. I will not go with you."

The minions shouted, "Resistance is futile, boy. If you don't comply, we will have to take you by force."

Markandeya ignored them, continuing his worship. Frustrated, the minions tried to pull him away, but no matter how hard they tried, they couldn't lift him. "We must inform YamaDev," they said to each other, and left.

Back in Yamalok, the minions approached YamaDev. "What! You've returned empty-handed?" Yama thundered.

The minions explained, "Deva, that boy possesses an unusual power. We were overwhelmed."

Yama said, "Alright, if it requires my intervention, I will handle it myself."

YamaDev, along with his minions, went to Markandeya. Seeing Yama approaching, Markandeya embraced the Shivaling tightly and began chanting, "Aum Namah Shivaya."

YamaDev laughed, "What? Do you think you can escape death? Your efforts are in vain! I am the mighty God of Death, and I have come personally to take you."

Determined to fulfill his duty, Yama threw his lasso at Markandeya, binding both the boy and the Shivaling together.

YamaDev pulled with all his strength, but he could not move Markandeya. Finally, in a last attempt, Yama hurled his weapon at the boy.

Suddenly, Lord Shiva emerged from the Shivaling, radiating with divine splendor. The sheer brilliance of his appearance blinded Yama. Infuriated, Shiva opened his third eye, and a beam of fire shot out, reducing YamaDev to ashes. It was through this event that Shiva earned the title "Mrityunjaya" (Conqueror of Death). Terrified, Yama's minions fled.

Shiva turned to Markandeya and said, "My dear devotee, I am immensely pleased with your devotion. You no longer need to fear death. You will remain sixteen years old forever."

With that blessing, Shiva disappeared. Markandeya's parents were overjoyed to see their son return unharmed.

However, the absence of YamaDev threw the universe into chaos. Without the God of Death, no one could die, and immortality disturbed the balance of life. The Devas and Maharshis approached Lord Shiva and pleaded with him, "Oh God of All, please forgive YamaDev for his actions. He will no longer harm your devotees."

Moved by their plea, Shiva restored Yama to life. From that day onward, YamaDev became extremely cautious when dealing with Lord Shiva's devotees.

42

THE KING'S WISH

In the ancient kingdom of Tirukkoyilur in Tamil Nadu, there lived a king named Meiporul Nayanar, a devout and pious follower of Lord Shiva. He served Shiva faithfully, not only in temples but also by caring for Shiva's devotees. The king regularly organized grand Yagas in Shiva temples.

Under the influence of Shaivism, the kingdom flourished in both the sciences and the arts. However, the prosperity of Tirukkoyilur made Muthanathan, the king of a neighboring kingdom, deeply resentful. Envious of their success, Muthanathan attacked Tirukkoyilur multiple times, but each time, he was defeated by Meiporul's army. Realizing he could never defeat Meiporul by fair means, Muthanathan devised a devious plan to destroy both the king and his kingdom.

Disguising himself as a Shaiva ascetic, Muthanathan entered Tirukkoyilur. Respecting the appearance of a Shaiva saint, the guards allowed him through to Meiporul's castle. Muthanathan made his way deeper into the palace, finally reaching the king's bedchamber, which was guarded by Dathan.

Muthanathan said, "Guard, let me through. I must meet the king."

Dathan replied, "No, I cannot. His Highness is asleep."

Muthanathan insisted, "Can't you see who I am? How dare you prevent a Shaiva Yogi from fulfilling his duty? I have come to teach the king the knowledge needed to attain Moksha. It is for his own benefit."

Dathan, convinced by the Yogi's claim, said, "If that is so, then very well."

Muthanathan was allowed into the king's chamber. Meiporul's wife awoke and saw the Yogi entering.

She said, "Dear, wake up. Someone has come to see you."

Muthanathan interjected, "I have come to impart the secret knowledge of Moksha, which was bestowed upon me by Lord Shiva himself. I need privacy with the king. You must leave."

Following the king's orders, the queen and the guards left. Meiporul then said, "Come, revered saint. Please sit here." He placed Muthanathan on a high seat, while he sat humbly at the ascetic's feet.

Muthanathan smirked and said, "Oh, you are indeed a devout soul. But how unfortunate, for you will not live much longer."

With that, Muthanathan pulled a dagger hidden within a scroll and stabbed the king. Meiporul collapsed in pain. Dathan, who had been suspicious of the Yogi's intentions from the start, had been hiding nearby. Hearing the commotion, he rushed into the chamber and attacked the false ascetic. Just as Dathan was about to strike Muthanathan with his sword, Meiporul, though grievously wounded, cried out, "Stop! Do not harm him. He is a Shaiva, and therefore he is connected to me. I command you to ensure the Yogi's safe passage to the borders of the kingdom. Dathan, you are responsible for his protection."

Unaware of the Yogi's true identity, Meiporul's orders were carried out. Despite learning of the king's injury, the king's subjects prepared to retaliate against the false ascetic, but Dathan intervened. "No one should harm him! I have direct orders from the king to let him go unharmed."

Dathan escorted Muthanathan out of the city and left him in a desolate forest, saying, "I know you are a false Shaiva. Unfortunately, the king is unaware of the truth. You are free to go now, but you will pay for your actions in the end."

Afterward, Dathan returned to the king and reported, "Your Highness, I have personally escorted the Shaiva to a place where no one can harm him."

Meiporul, weak but still composed, said, "Thank you, Dathan. Summon my ministers, my wife, and my kin to my deathbed. I wish to advise them on how to continue propagating Shaivism for the welfare of future generations."

Meiporul closed his eyes and meditated on Lord Shiva. Suddenly, Shiva appeared before him in all his magnificence. Shiva said, "Dear Meiporul, I am truly pleased with your devotion and faith. You forgave an offender who harmed you, believing him to be a Shaiva. Because of your unwavering devotion, you will attain Moksha. You will live to witness your legacy flourish."

Shiva blessed him and disappeared. Meiporul Nayanar went on to inspire Shaivism in neighboring kingdoms, and his descendants became ardent followers of Shiva, eventually establishing a mighty empire.

43

MURTHI'S REVOLUTION

In the ancient Pandyan Kingdom, there lived a humble devotee of Lord Shiva named Murthi, a member of the Vaishya (merchant) caste. By profession, Murthi was a merchant, but his devotion to Shiva was his true calling. Every day, he would offer aromatic sandalwood paste to anoint the idol of Lord Shiva in the famous Meenakshi Temple in Madurai.

For a time, the kingdom and its Shaiva subjects flourished under the influence of Shaivism. However, their fortune took a turn when the Pandyan Kingdom was invaded by northern attackers. The invaders successfully conquered the land, and the new king, a staunch follower of Jainism, took control.

One day, the Jaina king issued a public proclamation: "Citizens, you have witnessed the change of rule in the kingdom. Now, I must inform you of further changes. From this day forward, the kingdom will follow Jain principles. Every subject must convert to Jainism, or they will face the consequences."

Under his rule, the Shaivas were persecuted, and efforts to convert them to Jainism were relentless. Despite the pressure, Murthi remained steadfast in his devotion, continuing to offer sandalwood paste to Lord Shiva at the Meenakshi Temple.

The Jain king soon learned of Murthi's unwavering devotion and became threatened by his influence. Fearing that Murthi's actions could inspire resistance and jeopardize his throne, the king summoned his ministers. "I have heard of a Shaiva in the region who dares to defy my orders. He continues to worship his Shiva. Simply killing him would damage my reputation among the people. What should we do?"

One of the ministers suggested, "It is said that Murthi never fails to offer sandalwood paste to the Shiva idol in the temple. If we cut off his access to sandalwood, he will be forced to abandon his practice, either dying of regret or converting to Jainism."

The king, intrigued by the idea, replied, "Good. Block the supply of sandalwood to the city. Let us see how this Shaiva continues his service without it."

The very next day, the king ordered the complete cessation of sandalwood supply to the capital, confiscating whatever remained in the market. That morning, when Murthi went to his usual vendor and asked, "Brother, can you sell me some sandalwood for my divine offering?" the vendor replied, "Haven't you heard? Sandalwood is no longer available. The authorities have blocked its supply."

Murthi was shocked. "Oh God! Where else can I find sandalwood?"

The vendor explained, "You would have to travel far from here, at least a week's journey to find any."

Distressed, Murthi thought, "Oh Lord Shiva, I have spent my entire life offering you sandalwood paste. But now, I must find another way. I hope you will accept a different offering, one that resembles the color of sandalwood. My own skin."

Determined to continue his service, Murthi began using his own elbow, grinding it on a stone to create a paste from his flesh to anoint Lord Shiva. As he did so, his skin peeled away, his bones were exposed, and he began to bleed.

Suddenly, Lord Shiva appeared before Murthi and declared, "My dear devotee, I am deeply pleased by your unwavering devotion. I assure you that the tyrant king will soon meet his end, and a righteous person will be chosen to rule the kingdom."

As prophesied, the cruel king died the very next day, leaving no heir to the throne. To select a new ruler, the ministers followed the kingdom's tradition by sending out a royal elephant, adorned with a garland, to choose the next king. The blindfolded elephant roamed the city until it arrived at the Meenakshi Temple, where Murthi was deep in prayer to Lord Shiva. To everyone's surprise, the elephant placed the garland around Murthi's neck and bowed before him, signifying that he was to be the next king.

The crowd and ministers quickly approached Murthi, proclaiming, "According to tradition, you are now the rightful ruler of this land."

Murthi, who had never sought power or kingship, humbly addressed the people, "My fellow citizens, I am but a simple servant of Lord Shiva. I have never desired any position of authority. However, I see this as a divine command from Lord Shiva himself, and I accept this responsibility."

The people erupted in cheers, grateful for the end of the tyrannical reign of the previous king. The royal elephant lifted Murthi onto its back and carried him to the palace.

Once crowned king, Murthi summoned his ministers and decreed, "Reestablish the temples dedicated to Lord Shiva. Those who were forced to abandon Shaivism must be allowed to return to their original faith. Restore the supply of sandalwood to the city."

The ministers faithfully carried out his orders, and the kingdom once again became a center for Shaivism. Murthi ruled with humility, choosing to dress not in royal garments but as a devout Shaiva, his body smeared with sacred ash, adorned with Rudraksha beads and his hair matted in the traditional style. He rejected the luxuries of the crown and governed the land with fairness and devotion. Through diplomacy and influence, he spread the teachings of Shaivism far and wide, restoring peace and spiritual prosperity to the kingdom.

44

ADI SHANKARA'S ENCOUNTER

In the 8th century CE in India, there lived a great philosopher and sage named Adi Shankara, renowned for consolidating the doctrine of Advaita Vedanta. Shankara was born at a time when Hinduism was facing the increasing influence and imperialism of Buddhism and Jainism. He famously articulated the key difference between Hinduism and Buddhism by explaining that Hinduism asserts "Atman (Soul, Self) exists," while Buddhism teaches that there is "no Soul, no Self."

Shankara traveled extensively across the Indian subcontinent, spreading his philosophy through discourses and debates with masters of other religions. During one of his journeys, he stopped in Kashi (Varanasi), a prominent center of learning, to engage in theological discussions with local philosophers.

One summer day, Adi Shankara and his disciples were on their way to bathe in the sacred river Ganga when they encountered a Chandala (an outcaste from the Sudra group) leading four dogs on leashes. The Chandala, wearing ragged clothes and appearing unkempt, blocked the narrow path that Shankara and his followers were walking along.

Realizing that there was no way to avoid him, Shankara shouted, "Hey Chandala, move aside with your dogs and let us pass!"

The Chandala appeared to ignore him, continuing forward on the same path. Frustrated, Shankara called out again, "Halt, Chandala! Step aside and let us through!"

To Shankara's astonishment, the Chandala burst into a loud laugh and then, speaking in perfect Sanskrit, said, "Sir, whom are you asking to move aside? Are you asking the Self to move, or the body? You know that the Self is omnipresent, pure, and beyond action. And if you are speaking of the body, then you must know that the body is mere matter, lifeless on its own. How can it move of its own accord? Moreover, in what way is your body different from mine? If you truly understand the Supreme Truth of non-duality, you should know there is no distinction between a Chandala and a Brahmin. Are the moon reflected in the ocean and the moon reflected in a small bowl of water different from each other? Is not every being in the universe one and the same?"

Hearing these words, Adi Shankara was struck with both amazement and humility. He realized that this was no ordinary Chandala, but a divine revelation. Overcome with enlightenment, Shankara folded his palms, bowed, and touched the feet of the Chandala. He said, "One who sees all beings with the vision of oneness and lives in harmony with that truth is truly my teacher. O revered Chandala, you are my Guru. Please forgive my earlier ignorance."

At that moment, the Chandala and the four dogs vanished into thin air, and in their place, Lord Shiva appeared, resplendent in his divine form, holding the four Vedas in his hands. Shankara realized that the Chandala was none other than Lord Shiva in disguise, and the four dogs represented the four Vedas.

Filled with devotion, Adi Shankara prostrated himself at Shiva's feet and began to sing his praises: "I meditate on the Great God, the Lord of all, the destroyer of evil. I seek refuge in Him, the eternal, the all-auspicious, the Supreme."

Pleased by Shankara's devotion, Lord Shiva spoke, "My son, I am deeply content with your devotion. You are destined to reestablish Sanatana Dharma. You will have the power to give a flawless exposition of Advaita Vedanta and dispel the false doctrines that lead men toward duality and ignorance. Preach the Vedic faith and make it accessible to all. In the end, you will be united with me."

After blessing him, Lord Shiva disappeared. Following Shiva's instructions, Adi Shankara fulfilled his mission, reestablishing the Vedic faith throughout India. Many followers of Buddhism and Jainism reconverted to their original faith, and their places of worship were restored to the Vedic tradition.

45

THE UNINVITED GUESTS

In ancient Tamil Nadu, there lived a Brahmin named Somasimarar, a devout follower of Lord Shiva. Somasimarar was a temple priest by profession and led his life in true Shaiva fashion, embracing the belief that all beings are one. He lived with his wife, Susheela.

Somasimarar wished to perform a Yaga in honor of Lord Shiva and hoped that Shiva himself would attend and accept the offerings. To make this happen, he needed the help of Sundarar, a renowned Shaiva saint known for his ability to communicate directly with Shiva. However, Sundarar was suffering from a cold at the time. Concerned, Somasimarar sent him traditional medicines every day.

Sundarar's wife informed him about the person who had been sending the medicine. Curious and grateful, Sundarar met Somasimarar and asked, "Oh fellow Shaiva, you have been helping me with medicines for the past few days. How can I repay your kindness?"

Somasimarar replied, "Respected Sundarar, I wish to conduct a Yaga in honor of Lord Shiva and humbly request the Lord's presence at the event. Only you have the power to call him on my behalf."

Sundarar agreed, saying, "Of course, I will help you."

That same day, Sundarar prayed to Shiva, and the Lord appeared before him.

"What do you seek, my beloved devotee?" Shiva asked.

Sundarar replied, "Oh Lord Almighty, a fellow Shaiva, Somasimarar, is conducting a Yaga in your honour and has requested your presence."

Shiva smiled and said, "Alright, I will attend with my family."

After blessing Sundarar, Shiva disappeared.

Somasimarar scheduled the Yaga for a chosen date, and scholars and sages from distant places gathered, eager to participate, especially after hearing that Lord Shiva himself would attend. On the day of the Yaga, Shiva arrived in the guise of a Sudra family, accompanied by his wife Parvati and sons, Ganesha and Kartikeya.

The presence of a family from a lower caste at such a sacred ritual was seen as an affront, and the guests were outraged.

"The sanctity of this Yaga is ruined!" one guest shouted.

"I'm leaving," another added.

Somasimarar was disheartened by the reaction of his guests but felt unable to confront them. Despite this, he welcomed the Sudra family with great respect and offered them food.

"Please come in. The Yaga is about to begin, and we are awaiting Lord Shiva," he said to them.

The other guests were shocked by Somasimarar's behavior. They had never expected a Brahmin to treat a Sudra family with such kindness.

Suddenly, the Sudra family revealed their true forms, transforming into Lord Shiva, Parvati, Ganesha, and Kartikeya. The guests were overjoyed and awestruck at the sight of the divine family.

Shiva spoke, "You must treat everyone equally, regardless of caste or clan. The outer body is merely a disguise, but the soul within is the ultimate truth. Dear Somasi, I am pleased with your devotion. You are a true Shaiva, and your legacy will be a magnificent one."

After blessing Somasimarar, Lord Shiva and his family disappeared. The guests, having witnessed the truth, vowed never to discriminate against anyone based on caste again.

46

SPIDER'S VENOM

In the Chola Kingdom of South India, there lived a Brahmin named Tiruneelanakka, who served as the priest of the Ayavantheeswarar Shiva Temple. His primary duty was to recite the Vedas in the temple, and over time, he became an expert in Vedic scriptures. As a devout follower of Lord Shiva, Tiruneelanakka was known for his humility and service to Shiva's devotees, washing their feet and welcoming them into his home with great reverence.

One day, Tiruneelanakka and his wife went to the temple to perform their daily rituals. While Tiruneelanakka was deeply engrossed in reciting the Vedas and worshipping the Shivalinga, a spider fell from its web onto the sacred idol. Tiruneelanakka didn't notice, but his wife did. Concerned that the spider's venom might defile the Shivalinga, she blew it away. Taking further action, she spat on the spot where the spider had fallen and rubbed it away, following the traditional practice of spitting on a child's skin where a spider had landed to prevent the spread of venom. Although this act had no scientific or medical basis, it was done out of genuine concern.

When Tiruneelanakka saw what she had done, he was horrified and shouted, "What have you done, you fool? You spat on the sacred Shivalinga!"

His wife replied, "I did it to ensure the spider's venom didn't remain on the Shivalinga."

Angrily, Tiruneelanakka retorted, "Spider venom? Are you out of your mind? Even if a spider fell, you've polluted the sacred Shivalinga with your saliva! Don't you know spitting is disgraceful? There are proper rituals in the scriptures to cleanse the idol. Such primitive methods should never be used on divine icons!"

To rectify what he saw as a serious offense, Tiruneelanakka performed rituals to purify the Shivalinga and offered special prayers to Lord Shiva, seeking forgiveness. Afterward, he confronted his wife and said, "You have committed a grave sin by defiling the holy idol. I can no longer accept you as my wife. You must return to your parents and live with them."

Heartbroken, his wife stayed at the temple, weeping.

That night, while his wife slept in the temple, Tiruneelanakka returned to his home and went to sleep. In a dream, Lord Shiva appeared before him.

Shiva asked, "Tiruneelanakka, where are you?"

Confused, Tiruneelanakka replied, "Oh Lord, what has happened to you?"

To his shock, Shiva's appearance was unusual, while part of his body looked normal, the rest appeared affected by some sort of skin disorder.

Shiva explained, "My dear devotee, I have been afflicted by the venom of a spider. The only part of me that was healed is where your wife applied her saliva and rubbed it away. If she had continued, I would have been fully cured. But alas, you stopped her."

With these words, Shiva vanished, and Tiruneelanakka awoke from his dream, filled with realization. He understood that true devotion and love were superior to rigid rituals and that Shiva had gone to great lengths to show him this truth. Humbled, Tiruneelanakka rushed to the temple and called for his wife.

"My beloved wife, I am deeply sorry. Please forgive me. I now understand that God values sincere devotion from the heart more than adherence to rules and rituals. Lord Shiva himself has shown me this. Please accept my apologies and return home."

Tiruneelanakka's wife forgave him, and they returned home together. From that day forward, Tiruneelanakka became a true Shaiva, serving all with love and devotion, rather than focusing solely on ritualistic practices.

47

CURE OF A SHAIVA

A king named Manimudi once ruled the ancient Chola Kingdom with its capital at Pazhayannai. He was a devout follower of Lord Shiva and passed this devotion on to his daughter, Mangayarkkarasiyar, affectionately called Mani. As Mani grew into a beautiful woman, her father began searching for a suitable husband for her.

Meanwhile, in the neighboring Pandya Kingdom, there was a king named Nadumaran, also known as Koonpandyan (with "Koon" meaning hunchback). Though he had a physical deformity, Koonpandyan was renowned for his scholarly wisdom and mastery of warfare. Recognizing his skills, Manimudi arranged a diplomatic marriage between his daughter Mani and Koonpandyan. The wedding was a grand celebration attended by kings and dignitaries from many regions. After the ceremony, Mani left the Chola Kingdom and moved to the Pandya Kingdom with her new husband.

Upon arriving in Pandya, Mani was shocked to find a kingdom heavily influenced by Jainism. Shiva temples had been converted into Jain temples, and Jain priests and sages dominated the court. To her dismay, she soon discovered that her husband, King Koonpandyan, was a follower of Jainism.

One day, Koonpandyan summoned Mani and said, "I see you always wear the *Vibhuti* (sacred ash). But you must understand, this kingdom follows Jain traditions and you should not wear it in honor of Lord Shiva."

This left Mani heartbroken, feeling that her life was falling apart. However, she found comfort in one ally. Kulachirayar, a minister in the Pandya Kingdom was a devout Shaiva like her. Desperate to return her husband to the Shaiva faith, she approached Kulachirayar and confided, "We must bring Nadumaran back to Shaivism, no matter what it takes."

Kulachirayar agreed but cautioned, "Yes, it is the true path. But we must be discreet. If others discover our intentions, they will plot against us."

Together, they sent trusted messengers to search for someone who could help in their mission. Eventually, word reached them about a powerful and influential Shaiva sage named Thirugyana Sambandar, who traveled across the land preaching Shaivism. The queen immediately dispatched her emissaries to invite the sage to their kingdom.

Mani and Kulachirayar personally met Sambandar in Madurai. Mani pleaded, "The situation is dire. We urgently need your help, Your Holiness."

Sambandar responded, "I am well aware of the situation. The decline of Shaivism in the Pandya Kingdom has troubled me deeply. I have devoted my life to restoring Shaivism, and I would be honoured to assist in your mission."

With great reverence, the queen and the minister escorted Sambandar to the Pandya palace. Meanwhile, the Jain ministers, having heard of Sambandar's arrival, warned Koonpandyan, "Your Majesty, this Shaiva known as Thirugyana Sambandar is preaching against our religion. We cannot allow this to continue. If he is not stopped, Shaivism will regain dominance and Jainism will be wiped out. We must put an end to this immediately."

Koonpandyan asked, "What do you suggest we do?"

The Jain ministers advised, "We should burn down the settlement where Sambandar is staying. Once the fire spreads, the Shaivas will flee in fear and the threat to Jainism will be eliminated."

With the king's approval, the settlement where Thirugyana Sambandar and his disciples were staying was set on fire. The flames quickly spread, but fortunately, Sambandar and his followers narrowly escaped. Using his divine insight, Sambandar realized that the attack had been ordered by King Koonpandyan. Angered by this, Sambandar cursed the king, saying, "You will be afflicted by a rare and terrible disease."

The next morning, Queen Mani woke to find her husband stricken with a mysterious disease that covered his body in painful boils. The sight of the king's disfigured skin terrified the castle's servants, causing many to flee in fear. Koonpandyan was left unable to walk or even stand. The royal physicians hurried to treat him, but their efforts were in vain, and his condition continued to deteriorate.

Desperate, Koonpandyan summoned the Jain ministers and commanded them, "Cure me with your faith."

The ministers applied their herbs and offered prayers, but nothing worked. As his suffering worsened, Koonpandyan reflected, "I am being punished for my cruel actions against Thirugyana Sambandar. Only Sambandar can save me now."

Upon hearing this, Queen Mani invited Sambandar to the castle to heal her husband. She also had the king publicly announce, "I will follow the spiritual path of whoever can cure me of this deadly disease."

Sambandar arrived at the castle without delay. As soon as he stepped inside, the king felt a slight relief from his pain. Sambandar asked Mani to bring a golden seat and place it near the king. As he sat down, the king's rivals, angered by Sambandar's presence, rushed in and began to argue with him.

Mani intervened, shouting, "Dear followers of different paths, if you have any ideological disagreements with His Holiness Thirugyana Sambandar, I ask you to save them for after he has cured our beloved king!"

One of the Jain physicians boldly declared, "I will prove the Shaiva wrong. I will cure the king myself."

The physician sat across from Sambandar and attempted to treat the king. But despite his efforts, nothing changed, and the king remained in agony. With a calm smile, Sambandar took some Vibhuti and gently spread it over the king's body. Miraculously, the areas touched by the ash immediately began to heal. Sambandar continued his treatment and soon the king was completely cured of his affliction.

Overwhelmed with gratitude, Koonpandyan said to Sambandar, "Your path is the true one."

Hearing this, the Jain ministers grew furious and shouted, "Debate us on the sciences!"

Sambandar agreed and a public debate ensued. The Jains were swiftly defeated, unable to counter Sambandar's wisdom. After the debate, Koonpandyan made a public declaration: "I have embraced the true path of Shaivism. Lord Shiva is the one and only Supreme God. I encourage my subjects to follow the same path."

Following this, many Jains either converted to Shaivism or fled the kingdom. A few fanatics, unable to bear the humiliation of their defeat, tragically chose to end their own lives.

48

ELIXIR FOR INSANITY

In the 18th century, near a place called Alappuzha in Kerala, there was a grove close to the ruins of an ancient Vishnu temple, which had been destroyed by Muslim invaders from the north. The area lay abandoned for centuries until members of a local tribe began to visit frequently to hunt turtles in a nearby pond. They would hunt by immersing pointed sticks into the water; if a turtle was present, they could tell by the resistance of the stick.

One day, while a tribal woman was searching for turtles, she struck her stick against something unusual in the pond.

Although she was certain she had hit something hard, blood began to surface in the water. Panicking, she rushed to alert the others.

Soon, the entire village gathered to witness the mysterious phenomenon. They were astonished to see the pond covered in blood. "We must drain the pond to find the source," the villagers declared. Thus, they worked tirelessly for three days and nights to empty the pond. Even though they couldn't completely deplete it, they discovered the source of the bleeding: a cylindrical rock that continued to stream blood.

On the fourth day, a stranger appeared unexpectedly. Clad in Shaiva attire, he announced, "This is not an ordinary rock; it is a mighty and divine Shivaling. Empty the pond completely so that the base of the Shivaling is visible to all. If you establish a temple here based on this Shivaling, it will bring immense wealth and prosperity to this place. I will stop the bleeding right now."

With that, the stranger jumped to the spot and applied Vibhuti to the cracked part of the rock. Miraculously, the bleeding stopped. However, when the villagers tried to find the stranger afterward, he had vanished without a trace, as if he had disappeared into thin air. The villagers believed that he might have been Lord Shiva himself in disguise.

About a hundred years later, the temple, now known as the Thiruvizha Mahadeva Temple, had become quite popular. It employed many priests, administrative staff and cleaning crews, including a Nair man whose livelihood depended on his job there. Being a devotee of Shiva, he was grateful for his position.

Unfortunately, a mentally unstable stranger began to frequently visit the temple, harassing both devotees and staff. The Nair suffered the most; the unstable man even physically attacked him. Desperate and depressed, Nair hesitated to go to the temple, fearing for his safety. However, he resolved, "Lord Shiva has a solution for every problem. I must seek his help."

The next day, Nair went to the Thiruvizha temple and prayed, "Oh Lord Shiva, the Supreme God, the God of All, I can no longer endure the harassment from this man. I request your guidance in resolving this issue."

That night, Nair had an unusual dream in which Lord Shiva appeared and said, "Dear devotee, do not worry about your troubles at the temple. Just follow my instructions. Tomorrow evening, tie up the insane man when he comes to the temple. You will need to find the leaves of an extraordinary plant in the nearby thicket. Give these leaves to the priests of the temple and instruct them to crush them and mix them with some milk. They should perform a Puja on the mixture. Afterward, give this potion to the unstable man and after an hour, feed him rice porridge. He will begin to vomit, and then you should feed him the offerings from the temple's Puja and milk porridge. After that, he will no longer be a threat, so you can untie him and let him go. If he feels hungry, feed him rice."

Suddenly, Nair woke up from the dream, filled with joy and bliss, believing that Lord Shiva had spoken to him. The next day, he shared the divine instructions with the temple authorities, who followed them precisely. Remarkably, it worked: the man with the mental disability was cured as a result of the guidance given to Nair in his dream.

Word of the miracle spread throughout Kerala and soon the temple was flooded with devotees bringing their mentally ill relatives to seek help. Following the treatment prescribed by God, many were cured, including those who had arrived in chains. They returned home with their minds restored. As the temple flourished, the village thrived, transforming the area into a significant pilgrimage center.

49

CHANGE OF FATE

During the late 19th century in British Malabar, there lived a Namboodiri (a Brahmin of Kerala) who was an ardent devotee of Shiva. At the age of thirty-two, he became extremely depressed about his inevitable fate. According to a horoscope written by an astrologer long ago, the Namboodiri would die soon at this age. "I can't find decent sleep anymore because of these worries," he thought. "Maybe the horoscope is wrong. I need to validate it."

Thus, the Namboodiri traveled to Kaniyar, who lived in a place called Pazhoor. Kaniyar was renowned for his astrological skills and could predict anything. The Namboodiri hoped that if Kaniyar could confirm the authenticity of his horoscope and declare it false, he could live in peace without any worries.

By evening, the Namboodiri reached Kaniyar's house. Upon seeing him, Kaniyar felt troubled. He thought, "Dear Lord, I can sense death in the Namboodiri's face. He won't live a day longer; he will meet his end within hours. But how can I reveal this to him? How will he face the truth? I must find a way to avoid this."

The Namboodiri presented Kaniyar with some bananas and said, "Oh Kaniyar, I have come to seek your esteemed guidance. I bring my old horoscope, which predicts that I will die any time soon. I request you to check its accuracy."

Kaniyar paused for a moment before replying, "Dear Namboodiri, it is about to get dark. Why don't you return tomorrow morning? I will check it and even write a new horoscope for you."

The Namboodiri agreed, "You are right; it is getting dark. I will return tomorrow. Thank you for considering my request."

Convinced that the Namboodiri would die that night and that he wouldn't have to face him again, Kaniyar felt relieved as the naive Namboodiri left his house. He went straight to a nearby Shiva temple known as Perumthrikovil. There, he bathed in the temple pond and chanted his usual prayers to Shiva. Suddenly, it started to rain, and he struggled to find a dry place to stay. The temple was in ruins, having collapsed due to past incidents. Some hundred years ago, the Malabar region had been attacked by the Muslim invader Tipu Sultan, who destroyed many temples to establish his influence.

The Namboodiri felt sorrowful at the sight. "Such an auspicious temple of Shiva, yet it lies in ruins. It is unfortunate that it is in such a sorry state," he thought. He left the temple and went to his friend's house nearby to spend the night. However, he couldn't sleep, troubled by the temple's miserable condition. He pondered, "By the blessings of God, I am a wealthy man. But what use is this wealth if I cannot benefit others? I must rebuild the Perumthrikovil Shiva temple. I will spend my entire fortune if necessary."

Morning arrived, and the Namboodiri returned to the temple. After bathing in the pond and praying, he went back to Kaniyar's house. Kaniyar was astounded to see him. He thought, "Oh God! This is indeed a miracle! This person should have been dead by now. But I can sense some divine intervention; there is a holy aura surrounding him."

Kaniyar asked, "Dear Namboodiri, you have done something extraordinary after leaving here last evening. What is it?"

The Namboodiri replied, "No, I haven't done anything special. I just went to the Shiva temple, bathed there, prayed for a while, and spent the night at my friend's house."

Kaniyar said, "That's not all. Perhaps you haven't done anything physically, but you have indeed accomplished something significant mentally."

The Namboodiri responded, "Oh, right. Last night, I made a decision. I realized that the Perumthrikovil Temple was in a miserable state, shattered in ruins. So, I resolved to reconstruct the temple to restore its glory. Fortunately, I have enough money to do so."

Kaniyar jumped with joy. "That's right! That's enough! I must tell you, respected Namboodiri, your previous horoscope was accurate. You were indeed meant to die last night. But your decision to rebuild the temple and invest your wealth in public welfare has changed your fate. There is no need to test your astrology anymore; you will live a long life."

Enchanted by Kaniyar's words, the Namboodiri left home and returned to Pazhoor with the money needed for the temple reconstruction. The Perumthrikovil Shiva Temple was restored to its former splendor. Devotees from all over Malabar came to pray there, and it is said that the Namboodiri lived to the age of one hundred.

50

LIFE SPAN OF LORD SHIVA

In this book, you have read stories of Shiva that span from the beginning of the universe to the late 19th century CE. You may be wondering about the lifespan of Shiva. When discussing figures like Krishna, we can confidently say he lived during the Dwapara Yuga, while Sri Rama lived in the Treta Yuga. However, the time when Shiva lived remains unknown. Below, the lifespan of Shiva, Brahma, and Vishnu is explained.

As you know, the absolute Nirakara ParaBrahma manifested itself in different forms or avatars, similar to how we classify energy, such as mechanical, thermal, and nuclear energy.

Lord Shiva is one of the supreme forms of ParaBrahma's manifestation. In fact, Shiva was the first form to be manifested by ParaBrahma, which means that Shiva has existed since the very beginning.

Unlike gods such as Sri Rama and Krishna, who were avatars or human forms of the ultimate God, superior gods like Brahma, Vishnu, and Shiva exist eternally until the cycle of life ends, after which they are reborn.

It is believed that Shiva's lifespan is twice that of Vishnu's. Vishnu's lifespan is twice that of Brahma. Brahma lives for 100 Brahma years. So, what constitutes 1 Brahma year?

- 7.5 Nazhika = 1 Yama
- 4 Yama = Dawn to Dusk or Dusk to Dawn
- 8 Yama = 1 entire day
- 360 human years = 1 Deva year (Divya Varsh)
- 4800 Divya Varsh / 1,728,000 human years = 1 Satya Yuga
- 3600 Divya Varsh / 1,296,000 human years = 1 Treta Yuga
- 2400 Divya Varsh / 864,000 human years = 1 Dwapara Yuga
- 1200 Divya Varsh / 432,000 human years = 1 Kali Yuga
- 12,000 Divya Varsh / 4,320,000 human years = 1 Maha Yuga
- 1000 Maha Yugas = 1 Kalpa = 1 day (excluding night) of Brahma

(Note: 2 Kalpas constitute a day and night of Brahma, totaling 8.64 billion human years.)

In one day of Brahma, he performs the divine task of creation with the help of 14 Manus, one after the other. An era of Manu during which he reigns is called a Manvantara.

Currently, we are in the first day of Brahma's 51st year, and six Manus have completed their tasks. At present, the seventh Manu, named Vaivaswadan, is assisting Brahma in the act of creation. Everything that Brahma creates during the day will be destroyed at dusk.

As mentioned earlier, Brahma has a lifespan of 100 years. Once he dies, a new Brahma is born. It is said that millions of

Brahmas have been born and died before him. Additionally, it is said that 14 Indra Devas will be born and die one by one during each Brahma's life.

Therefore, Shiva exists above the Yugas. The Yugas represent a timescale of the human world, while Lord Shiva transcends that scale.

GLOSSARY

Adharma - Antonym of Dharma. It means 'that which is not in accord with the Dharma'

Amrit - Nectar or Ambrosia

Apsaras - Celestial nymphs.

Ashram - A hermitage, monastic community, or other place of religious retreat

Asura - A member of a class of divine beings in the Vedic period who tends to be evil

Avatar - A manifestation of a deity or released soul in bodily form on earth

Bael - Bael is used in the ritual rites of Hindus and is considered as one of the sacred trees of Hinduism.

Brahmin - A member of the Hindu caste, comprising of priests and Vedic scholars.

Deva - A member of a class of divine beings in the Vedic period who are benevolent

Devalok - Heavens

Dharma - The eternal law of the cosmos, inherent in the very nature of things

Dwapara Yuga - It is the third out of the four yugas, or ages of mankind. It follows the Satya Yuga and Treta Yuga and is followed by the Kali Yuga

Gandharva - Male nature spirits. They act as messengers between the gods and humans

Gowhatya - Killing a cow. As cow is a sacred animal in Hinduism, killing a cow is considered one of the worst sin.

Jyotirlinga - A Jyotirlinga is a devotional representation of Lord Shiva. Jyoti means 'radiance' and lingam the 'Image or Sign' of Shiva; Jyotir Lingam thus means the Radiant Sign of The Almighty Shiva

Kali Yuga - It is the fourth and final out of the four yugas, or ages of mankind. It follows the Satya Yuga, Treta Yuga and Dwapara Yuga

Kirata - Tribe of Mountain Dwellers

Krittikas - The personification of six stars as maidens. It is one of the clusters which makes up the constellation Taurus.

Kshatriya - A member of the military caste. The traditional function of the Kshatriyas is to protect society by fighting in wartime and governing in peacetime

Ksheera Sagara - Ocean of milk

Maya - Illusion

Moksha - Release from the cycle of rebirth impelled by the law of karma, the transcendent state attained as a result of being released from the cycle of rebirth.

Nagaraja - King of Nagas or Serpents

Panchaloha - A term for traditional five-metal alloys of sacred significance, used for making temple idols and jewelry

Patala - Refers to the subterranean realms of the universe – which are located under the earth. Patala is often translated as netherworld

Pranayama - Pranayama is a fundamental part of yoga involving controlled breathing.

Puja - The Act of Worship

Pura - Fortified City

Rakshasa - A malignant demon

Rishi/Maharshi - Sage

Satya Yuga - It is the first out of the four yugas, or ages of mankind. It is followed by the Treta Yuga, Dwapara Yuga and Kali Yuga

Sahasranama - Thousand names of a deity. Meant to be auspicious and divine

Samudra Manthan - Churning of the Ocean

Sanatanist - One who follows Sanatana Dharma i.e. the teachings of Hinduism.

Sat/Satya - Truth

Shaivism - It is one of the major traditions within Hinduism that reveres Shiva as the Supreme Being. The followers of Shaivism are called "Shaivites".

Shivaganas - Minions of Lord Shiva

Shivaling - An abstract representation of Lord Shiva, used for worship in temples, shrines, or as self-manifested natural objects

Sudra - A member of a Hindu caste, comprising of laborers and peasants. Most fundamental part of Hindu social structure as everyone else depends on Sudras as they provide food and workforce

Treta Yuga - It is the second out of the four yugas, or ages of mankind. It follows the Satya Yuga and is followed by the Dwapara Yuga and Kali Yuga

Trimurti - Trinity - Shiva, Vishnu and Brahma

Trishula - Trident

Vaishya - A member of a Hindu caste, comprising of merchants and farmers

Vanara - Beings with human characteristics but features of monkey.

Veda - Holy text of Hinduism, e.g. Rig Veda, Sama Veda, Yajur Veda, and Atharva Veda.

Vibhuti - Devotees apply vibhuti traditionally as three horizontal lines across the forehead and other parts of the body to honor Shiva.

Yajna/Yaga - Ritual

Yama - A Yama = 1/4 of a day or night. Eight Yamas make half of the day (either day or night)

Yamalok - The kingdom of YamaDev, the God of Death.

Yogi - Ascetic

Yojana - Vedic unit of measurement

Yuga - Eras of the World

BIBLIOGRAPHY

Maha Shiva Purana
Linga Purana
Brahma Purana
Padma Purana
Periya Purana
Aithihya Mala
Surya Siddhanta

www.ingramcontent.com/pod-product-compliance
Ingram Content Group UK Ltd.
Pitfield, Milton Keynes, MK11 3LW, UK
UKHW041351190726
13845UKWH00026B/542

9 788198 16756